REDCLIFFE
Sketch by Jane Williams

DEDICATION

To my wife Gerry
and sons Peter and Jonathan,
with love

and also

To the police horses I was privileged to partner:
Redcliffe, Mendip, Jubilee, Sulis,
Wansdyke and Steele

Horse, thou art truly a creature without equal;

For thou fliest without wings,

And conquerest without sword.

(from the Koran)

CONTENTS

ABOUT THE AUTHOR

Stephen Foulkes was born and educated in Bristol. He joined the Somerset Constabulary as a police cadet in 1965, and saw service in Taunton and Weston-super-Mare. He joined the regulars in 1967 and was the first officer posted into the city of Bath following the amalgamation into the Somerset and Bath Constabulary. While he was there he performed foot patrol duties, and after the inception of the unit beat policing scheme, became a panda car driver. He also volunteered to join the Force Underwater Search Unit, and remained a police diver for eight years until forced to give it up because, he says, his fins wouldn't fit through the stirrups! In 1971 he moved to Weston-super-Mare as a traffic patrol officer, and later policed the newly-opened M5 motorway. After the amalgamation of the Bristol and Somerset Forces into the Avon and Somerset Constabulary, he fulfilled a long-standing

The author Stephen Foulkes

ambition in 1975 by joining the Mounted Section in Bristol, where he remained until his retirement in 1996. He was promoted to sergeant in 1990. Since 1994 he has been a member of the Board of Directors of the Avon Riding Centre for the Disabled.

Since his retirement and the development of his semi-professional singing career into a full-time occupation, his bass-baritone voice has been in demand around the country. He has performed for choral societies in London, Edinburgh, Manchester, Bolton,

Epsom, Plymouth and Launceston, as well as many societies in the South West region. For ten years he was a bass lay-clerk with the Bristol Cathedral Choir, and has made many recordings and radio broadcasts. In 1985 he was invited to sing the solo Bach cantata *Ich Habe Genug* in Cologne as part of the city's Bach Tercentenary celebrations, and has since performed all over the continent and in the United States. His engagements include a ten year spell as bass soloist for the Bath Choral Society's performances of Handel's *Messiah*, presented annually in December in Bath Abbey; and in 1997 he was appointed judge and recitalist in a national competition for song composers. 1998 witnessed his debut as a solo performer in Bath's prestigious International Music Festival. He is a founder member of the Avon and Somerset Constabulary Male Voice Choir (for whom he still appears as soloist), the Bath Festival Chorus, and the prize-winning chamber choir, Bath Camerata.

His other interests include *la vie française* and sailing his Wanderer dinghy. He lives in Bristol with his wife Geraldine and two sons, Peter and Jonathan, both of whom have been members with him of the choir of St. Mary Redcliffe Church.

PREFACE

For many years the Mounted establishment of the Avon and Somerset Constabulary, based at Bower Ashton just outside Bristol, carried an information leaflet about the unit, which was handed out to any interested visitor. This leaflet proclaimed that the foundation of the police force's "oldest specialist unit" occurred in 1889, and in the years leading up to the "centenary" no-one doubted the validity of the date. During 1988 the Horsemaster Chief Inspector Peter Griffiths set about some research with a view to preparing something to mark the one hundred years' existence for the year 1989. However his initial research very quickly established that the accepted date was in error and the real date of foundation was in fact 1899.

A hard-pressed secretary had, in preparing the visitor's leaflet, accidentally mistaken the last two digits and the date was then accepted without question. When he discovered the error Peter Griffiths abandoned his research, no doubt anticipating that someone other than he would be around to prepare a suitable tribute for 1999. As a member of the Mounted Branch in Bristol since 1975, I had always been curious about the circumstances surrounding the foundation of the unit. Although official enthusiasm for the project diminished in 1988 as the centenary was still a decade away, my own interest had been kindled. As my retirement loomed, it occurred to me that I would be in an ideal position to carry on what had been abandoned in 1988. I felt very strongly that our one hundred years should be celebrated in a suitable way. As far as I knew, there was no record of the history of Bristol's Mounted Section, so it seemed that the most appropriate way to celebrate the event would be to write that history. I was further motivated by the recurring rumours circulating about this time, that the Branch was in danger of being disbanded. If the Force was to face the new century without a Mounted Section, I felt it even more appropriate that there should be some sort of record of our existence. I have also been encouraged by the enthusiasm for the project from colleagues past and present. Without their support and willingness to share their memories, the story of the past fifty years would have been sparse indeed, because the paucity of records meant that I had to rely greatly on their recollections. When the inevitable difficulties arose and I felt my own enthusiasm draining away, a chance conversation or comment from a colleague about the project would re-ignite the spark as I realised that they shared with me a desire to see the book through to completion.

Further encouragement came in the shape of the local media, with Radio Bristol providing air-time and the Bristol Evening Post news-space, to enable my appeal for information to be broadcast far and wide. Their interest in the project was greatly appreciated and resulted in many members of the public contacting me with their stories, which would otherwise have been lost.

I am particularly grateful to Mr David Shattock, CBE, OStJ, QPM, former Chief Constable of the Avon and Somerset Constabulary, for his interest in this book and for generously agreeing to write the Foreword. Thanks are also due in no small measure to the following friends and former colleagues for their enthusiastic assistance during my research period: Mrs Grace Bradley; Mr Kenneth Bush; Mr Anthony Clarke; Mrs Doreen Evans; Mr Graham Fowler; Mr Bill Hardacre; Mrs Janet Hunt; Mr James Marment; Mr Alan Milsom; Mr Ivor Morris; Mr Ronald Smith; and Mr Frank Turner. I am also indebted to the staff at the Bristol Record Office and at the Council House for their unfailing courtesy and assistance while I was researching in their offices.

Further thanks are due to Mrs C.J.Osborne, widow of former PC Michael Osborne, for permission to use extracts from Michael's book, *Policing Bristol* . In addition I am grateful to Mr. Brian Howell for similar access to his book, *The Police in Late Victorian Bristol*, and his study *The Development of the Bristol Police Force*. Their insights were invaluable to me in the early days as I sat down to try to commit what were then fairly incoherent thoughts to paper.

My thanks also go to my esteemed singing teacher and friend, Mollie Petrie, for her perusal of the text and helpful comments and hints for improvement, which I have accepted. Thanks too are due to my wife Gerry, mother Christine and sister Wendy Randall for scanning the first drafts and pointing out mistakes which I had overlooked. I am also very grateful to my publisher, Catherine Mason of Broadcast Books, for her initial and continuing encouragement, and her perceptive editing of the book. The interest shown by friends and former colleagues was also greatly appreciated. Any errors, incorrect admissions or glaring omissions can however be put down solely to me.

I apologise to any former colleagues who do not appear as individuals in the course of the narrative of this book. This is not because I consider them any less important in the development of the unit, but because I felt that a broader sweep would be more appropriate and more readable in the context than a succession of characters. Of course, every constituent member was an important part of the whole, and it was often the unsung officers who deserved the credit for maintaining a commitment to the job "on the streets" while others achieved a more high-profile reputation with appearances at Horse Shows. Anyone who contributed in any way to the efficient running of the Section was an equally valuable member.

Finally, I consider that I have been very fortunate in serving the majority of my career with the horses. I hope that the writing of this history will in part allow me to give back something for all the years of fascinating service I have enjoyed with them.

S.F.
BRISTOL, SEPTEMBER 1998

FOREWORD

The horse has been with us since the start of modern civilisation. It is a beast of burden and equally a beast of great beauty. It has been fought over by kings and countries, sultans and sheikhs, and is, of course, the centre of a great sporting industry.

The police horse has not been in use in all the forces of England and Wales, but here in the Avon and Somerset Constabulary it has had a treasured place for many years that continues to the present day. It is above all a valuable asset, which can do the work of 20 officers in public order situations. It can search vast areas of inhospitable country for missing persons, and not least of all it is a most valuable public relations asset.

Stephen Foulkes, the author of this book, was a most creditable police horseman and a very successful police ambassador. His book is written with great knowledge and great affection and I am delighted to offer this foreword today. I hope this book will provide many hours of enjoyment not only to the enthusiast of the horse, but also as a small part of the fabric of a developing society within the police service.

David Shattock CBE, O St J, QPM
Chief Constable, Avon and Somerset
Constabulary 1989-1998

INTRODUCTION

Ever since the third millennium BC, when Mankind first learnt to harness the horse's talents for his own use, the animal has been a major factor in many subsequent human achievements. It became a beast of burden, a form of transport, a model for art, a partner in sport and a conqueror in war. The physical and psychological advantages of its use against men on foot were quickly realised, and the horse became a vital element in the struggle for military and commercial domination between the nations of the world.

The Industrial Revolution, however, irrevocably changed the way the horse was used. By the end of the nineteenth century, the military and working horse had almost been rendered obsolete by the machinery of industrialisation, with all its attendant modernising influences. The advent of the internal combustion engine, which added mobility to power, completed the eclipse.

It is a curious feature of the British that they have retained an affection for horses which has outlived their practical usefulness in many areas of working life. The army maintained its troop of cavalry for ceremonial duties, and found a ready public audience for pageants involving the soldiers and their beautifully groomed horses. Some traders, merchants and breweries found that local distribution of their products could be just as cheaply and easily performed by horse and cart, and provided a considerable spin-off in positive advertising. The police service retained mounted units because of the very qualities which made the horse pre-eminent in battle. Its size, strength, mobility and sheer presence, allied to the public's respect for the animal, could be harnessed and used on the streets in assisting the police in many practical duties.

From the inception of the British Police Service in 1835, one of the basic precepts was that of "policing by consent". The power to enforce the law was delegated to police who were formed out of the community and for the community. Any method of individual or communal suppression had to be acceptable to the wider public, and the police were answerable for their actions to representative bodies made up from members of that community. (The representative body to whom Chief Constables were responsible was known as the Watch Committee, the oldest and most prestigious of the Council committees). It had never been an acceptable feature of policing to use brutality or overpowering strength to overcome disorder, but only the application of "as much force as is necessary to achieve the objective". It followed then that the use of what could be described as the more violent methods of crowd control would not be an acceptable option.

However, the problem of containing public disorder when it occasionally erupts has always challenged the civil authorities. Bristol itself had been the scene of riots in the past, notably in 1831, when the Reform Riots destroyed many buildings in central Bristol including the Bishop's Palace. These riots were a major influence in the foundation of a professional police service as it became apparent that some form of crowd control, and the ability to suppress disorder, had to be available to the British Police. To employ the advantages of mounted men was an obvious solution.

In order to utilise horses in performing these tasks, the animals had to be trained to accept circumstances which were not necessarily within their sphere of understanding. Apart from a gregarious herding instinct, the only defence nature gave the horse as protection from predators millions of years ago was that of flight - to run away from anything they heard or saw and did not understand. In response to this natural instinct, horses remain basically timid animals and often do not comprehend much of the environment in which man requires them to work. After recruitment into the police service (usually at rising 4 years of age when the animal had grown sufficiently to accept regular exercise without causing strain to its young bones, tendons and muscles), the horses had to undergo a basic training which was designed to overcome these instinctive reactions and encouraged them instead to respond to their riders commands, with the intention of finally producing quiet, obedient and well-balanced animals which were used to traffic, unusual sights and sounds and able to work alone or with other horses.

In addition to overcoming instinctive reactions, the horses had to be taught to stand, walk, trot and canter correctly, and also to perform what were for them unnatural movements: walking or trotting sideways (called the half-pass or the full-pass depending on the angle) and walking backwards (rein-back). All these manoeuvres enabled a mounted police officer to control a crowd by utilising the movements safely and effectively. In most circumstances the use of the ultimate sanction of a flat-out charge would not need to be exercised, and the mounted units could be used without recourse to the more violent alternatives.

From the very first days the Bristol unit adopted the old army policy of keeping a mounted man in partnership with his horse for long periods of time, with the intention of increasing their combined effectiveness by developing and maintaining the horse's confidence. When faced with circumstances which might frighten the animal, it is necessary for the officer to know how it is going to react in order to take appropriate action, and the horse will react more readily to the promptings of a rider it knows and trusts. Whatever the situation, even under the severe provocation often encountered in crowd disorders, the use of the horse and rider team had to be made as safe and effective as possible.

The history of the use of police horses has subsequently shown that original emphasis on "safe effectiveness" to be justified. In all the years police horses have been employed in crowd disorders in this country, there has not been a single death as a result of their use. There have been a few serious injuries sustained, as well as many minor ones, but in the circumstances of severe disorder this may be considered inevitable. Compared with riot suppression across the globe, which on many occasions involved the use of firearms with fatal consequences, incidents in this country have been relatively bloodless.

The priority of the branch has always been to try to keep the limit of force imposed by mounted units at an appropriate level. Avenues of escape are left open, so that the objective of splitting up a large crowd could be achieved without forcing people into potentially fatal corners. Where the objective was to move a generally well-behaved crowd for its own safety, then the height and vision of the mounted officer enabled police to perform these functions in relative safety.

The famous "white horse of Wembley" incident was a good example of this type of work. PC Scorey (who was a native of Bristol) and his horse *Billy* earned undying fame in 1923 when they were on duty at Wembley Stadium on the occasion of the first FA Cup Final to be staged there. King George V was present to watch the game, and from the royal box he looked down on an enormous crowd of over-excited spectators and rival fans who began to swarm over and through the turnstiles and barricades in spite of all the efforts of the foot police to prevent them. Within minutes the football pitch was completely obliterated, and it appeared that the football match of the year had become an impossibility. The police were powerless, and the air was charged with that terrifying emotion generated by an unruly mass of people. It was a moment when a trivial incident could flare up into a dangerous situation. Ten mounted police had arrived as reinforcements, but even they could not break their way through to the pitch. Then suddenly an officer on a big grey horse appeared, waving his arms to motion back the surging crowds while he guided the horse with his legs and rode forwards. PC Scorey and *Billy* were able to open up a space in which it was possible for his comrades to operate and follow his example. Eventually the King and players reached the pitch unhampered, and the historic match was completed. (Abridged from *Police Horses* by Judith Campbell)

Time and time again, the use of horses has been considered a valuable tool in assisting with the work of police forces across the country. This is the story of the Mounted Section in Bristol. When compared with Branches in London or Manchester it is a small unit, but it has maintained a high profile and an envied position amongst its peers. In addition to the more obvious police operations involving horses, there have been many community-related tasks to perform, and the goodwill thus generated has helped maintain the vital element of favourable police-public relations. I believe that the citizens of Bristol - and latterly the people of Avon and Somerset - have been proud of "their" police horses, and I hope that the relating of the unit's history in these few pages will help sustain that pride.

Police horses have been patrolling the streets of Bristol now for one hundred years, and in offering this history I salute them all.

CHAPTER ONE

FOUNDATION

In the years leading up to the end of the nineteenth century, the Police Force within the City and County of Bristol would have made as much use of real horsepower as the rest of contemporary society. Photographs of the age show the horse dominating every thoroughfare, street and lane, either drawing carriages, cabs or carts, or transporting individuals about their business. The police service owned horses which were required to pull prison vans, fire appliances, and as conveyances for senior officers, but no horses were specifically kept for mounted police as a unit. In spite of the fact that the "Bow Street Horse Patrol" had been operating in London since 1805, it seems that provincial forces such as Bristol's

13 working horses are visible in this Bristol scene, c.1899

did not regard a group of specially-trained mounted police officers as a necessary addition to the Constabulary's capabilities.

In a time when the ability to ride a horse was almost as common as today's ability to drive a car, use could be made of constables from amongst the ranks should mounted officers be required. These constables could well have joined the Force direct from a cavalry regiment of the British Army, although many could also have come from the farms in the region, where working with horses would have been second nature to them. Twenty years before the turn of the century, local traders had hired out their horses to the police service whenever the need arose. A precedent had already been set in this regard in 1877 when a Fire Brigade was formed within the City Police Force, consisting of 12 men who held the rank of First Class Constable, and one the rank of Sergeant.

The Watch Committee could not decide whether to maintain their own horses to draw the fire appliances or to hire them from a supplier. Eventually it was agreed to borrow horses from the Bristol Tramways and Carriage Co. Ltd., who would supply the horses for the Brigade for the sum £100 per annum, plus 10 shillings per horse borrowed. The Fire Brigade was eventually permitted to purchase their own horses in 1880, and animals were also acquired to draw the Prison Van. Similar arrangements regarding the borrowing of horses for other police uses seems to have been normal practice, with appropriate financial compensation being awarded.

In the late 1830s the Chartist Movement in London gave rise to street disorders, and the Horse Patrol there was mobilised for the first time to keep public order. They proved to be very successful at the task, and in addition they helped to regulate processions at ceremonial occasions and large gatherings. The temporary mounted police in Bristol would also have been involved on similar occasions. In March 1880 the Bristol Watch Committee minutes note that "Chief Constable Coathupe is authorised to employ as many Mounted men as he might consider necessary to assist in preserving order at the ensuing election". However, mounted duty remained a temporary and infrequent obligation for selected constables throughout the 1880s, although the authorities would have been well aware that the attendance of men on horseback at such events would assist in maintaining order. Indeed the early 1890s provided the local Watch Committee with plenty of evidence to this effect.

With the Trades Unions beginning to mobilise their members to improve working conditions, the potential for civil disorder increased. A serious labour dispute ensued toward the end of 1892, which initially involved members of the Bristol Dockers' Union, timber workers and quayside labourers, but soon encompassed other trades sympathetic to their cause. When blackleg "free labourers" were protected by the police in taking over the strikers jobs, a confrontation was inevitable. Matters came to a head when Mr. Ben Tillett, the General Secretary of the Dockers' Union, came to Bristol (his birthplace) with the purpose of organising a mass demonstration and march "to raise money for the starving families of the strikers". This so alarmed the Mayor, who felt the police force to be of insufficient strength to meet the challenge, that he wrote to the Home Secretary asking for military assistance.

The march was scheduled for 23rd December 1892, which later became known as "Black Friday". The day before the event two squadrons of troops comprising 200 Dragoons and Hussar Lancers entered the city from Aldershot. The Western Daily Press reported that Bristol was in a state of the greatest commotion, disorder and alarm when the march began. The Chief Constable, Mr. Edwin Coathupe, informed his Superintendents that "should a procession, crowd or mob perambulating the streets break into a run or make rushes to terrorise the citizens, the police must disperse it and if necessary arrest the principals".

Edwin Coathupe

The size of the crowd assembled in the Horsefair that night was 35,000, of which 5,000 took part in the march from Tower Hill. The route decreed by the police was soon abandoned, and great disorder ensued. The temporary mounted police, ten in number, were placed as a cordon in Prince Street under the command of Inspector Tanner. However the cordon was easily breached and attempts to turn back the demonstration proved futile. The crowd surged around them throwing stones and the mounted unit was largely ineffective.

Inspector Tanner later described the crowd as "riotous", and his command of temporarily mounted officers had neither the training nor the experience in either themselves or their horses to deal with the mêlée.

When the march reached the assembled mass in the Horsefair the scene developed into one of the greatest disorder and it became apparent that the police were powerless to do anything about it. Consequently the City Magistrate read the Riot Act, and when the crowd did not disperse, the military were brought in. They rode right through the crowd, scattering people all over the place. Many people were injured in the clash, but the cavalry was obliged to charge again before the objective was achieved. The strike leaders were arrested, and Ben Tillett himself later faced trial on a charge of incitement to riot. He was found not guilty at his trial in the Old Bailey the following April.

The City Magistrate was later obliged to defend his decision to call in the troops; he reminded his critics, with some justification, that the Mayor of Bristol had been put on trial for not doing so during the riots of 1831. The local press however judged that "there was nothing more than the police would have been able to deal with...it was a panic-stricken and needless appeal to military force". (Bristol Mercury, 24th December 1892)

The convulsion and activity of "Black Friday" would have provided a lesson not lost on the Watch Committee. It was obvious that the use of horses in containing public disorder was a valuable tool to have available. However, in the light of the subsequent criticism regarding the use of the cavalry, and the ineffectiveness of the untrained police mounted unit, it was equally clear that any mounted men employed should be properly organised and trained. When the question of establishing a full-time mounted unit arose six years later, many members would have retained memories of these incidents which may have influenced their decision.

Another factor leading to the formation of the Mounted Section occurred in 1897 when the boundary of the city extended to absorb districts as far flung as Stapleton, St.George and parts of Horfield, Westbury, Brislington and Bedminster. The policing of these outer districts, which now encompassed semi-rural areas, would have stretched the resources of a police force still predominantly on foot, and using horses to help overcome the policing problems was an obvious solution. Chief Constable Henry Allbutt considered that a Mounted Branch was essential to the efficient policing of the new districts, and to maintain effective communications.

But perhaps the final element that persuaded the Committee in favour of a full-time Branch was the use of the temporary mounted constables as escort for the civic dignitaries when they attended church services on formal occasions. It could be assumed that taking constables from beat duty, and horses from local traders, resulted in a less than impressive display - a report signed by the Chief Constable Henry Allbutt indicated as much when he also decried the condition of the saddlery!

The disreputable appearance of the escort, in full view of the city's dignitaries and populace, was a civic humiliation. Members of the Watch Committee found time to debate the situation, and the minutes of 26th April 1899 reported that it was: "Resolved that the Chief Constable report as to the desirability of having a mounted patrol and upon the condition of the present saddlery".

The minutes were signed by Herbert Ashman, the Mayor, who was Chairman of the Watch Committee. With horses being a common sight on the streets of Bristol, coupled with the occasions on which they were required to be hired, the resolution would not have been considered unusual in any way but passed during the course of ordinary business to correct a perceived deficiency.

Consequently on 17th May 1899 Henry Allbutt compiled a special report headed "Proposed Mounted Police":
The Chief Constable has the honour to report that in accordance with the instructions of the Committee he has examined the saddlery used by the Police when engaged upon escort duty. The Chief Constable finds that there are only three saddles belonging to the Corporation, and twelve sets of bridles, headstalls, etc, and twelve sabres. The sabres are in fair condition but the sad-

Henry Allbutt

dlery requires renewal. The Chief Constable would advocate the establishment of a small permanent mounted force of four constables, and for these plenty of employment could be found in patrol duty and in acting as mounted orderlies in carrying despatches between the Central, and the outside Police Stations... This number would not of course be sufficient for escort duty for which the ordinary police would have to be mounted as heretofore. The Chief Constable could provide these four men without asking for any increase of the Force. If the Mounted Branch were made larger he would have to ask for extra men. But whether a permanent mounted branch be established or not the Chief Constable would strongly recommend that new saddlery and appointments for one officer and eight men be purchased, so that when an escort is turned out it may not present the discreditable appearance which it does at present". The report was signed H. Allbutt, C.C.

One can detect in this report some subterfuge on the part of the Chief Constable! In it he advocates the foundation of a full-time Mounted Branch, but he indicates that he could only provide four officers if the Constabulary's strength was maintained at its then current level of 488 officers. He underlines the fact that this number will not be sufficient for escort duty, the very duty which prompted the report. He states plainly that if the Mounted Branch was made larger he would have to ask for extra men. He then goes on to say how many extra men he deemed suitable for a decent escort, and one can imagine him sitting back from his desk with a little smile in anticipation of an extension to his Force.

On 24th May 1899 his ambition was achieved. The Watch Committee minutes records that it: *"Read a report from the Chief Constable on the desirability of having a mounted patrol, and on the condition of the saddlery. Resolved - that new saddlery and appointments be provided for 1 officer and 8 men and it was resolved by 6 votes to 3 that four additional horses be purchased in accordance with the resolution of the Council of 12th July last. Herbert Ashman, Mayor"*.

It is interesting to note that this resolution is rather ambiguous in its support for the formation of a full-time Mounted Branch. It quite clearly agrees with the acquisition of saddlery and appointments "for 1 officer and eight men", but this could have been referring to officers of the "ordinary police" who provided men for the escort up until this time. The resolution to acquire four additional horses "in accordance with the resolution of the Council of 12th

July last" (1898) was referring to an expansion of the Fire Brigade in the City, and neither the minutes nor the press reports of the meeting mention the possibility of a permanent Mounted Branch.

In spite of the apparent ambiguity of the minutes, Henry Allbutt must have been given the authority either by the resolution of 24th May 1899 or another subsequently lost or unminuted, to form a Mounted Branch, and mention of the specific unit first appears in the Watch Committee minutes of 27th September 1899. Here it was recorded that tenders for the following was approved:

"*1 Mounted Inspector (Turner):*
Dress tunic
Dress trousers for riding 110/-
8 Mounted Men:
Cavalry tunics 24/6
Riding trousers 26/-
Sling belts 12/-"

From this time, records of specialist police horses begin to appear, while those relating to horses for prison vans and fire appliances gradually decrease and eventually disappear. The escorts could from henceforth adopt a more professional footing, with officers responsible for their own mounts and equipment. The Mounted Branch of the Bristol Constabulary could now commence their "*patrol duty, and in acting as mounted orderlies in carrying despatches between the Central, and the outside Police Stations*".

CHAPTER TWO

EARLY YEARS

In 1886 Liverpool was the first police force outside London to found a mounted unit following labour unrest in the city, and thirteen years later Bristol followed their example and became the second provincial mounted force of the country. With memories of the 1892 riot still fresh in the minds of the authorities, and taking into consideration the importance of the Victorian port, the move would have surprised no-one. But in spite of Home Office encouragement, there was no wholesale rush to set up such units around the country. Manchester (1900), Sheffield (1904), Lancashire (1911) and Durham (1913) all followed suit before the First World War, mainly in response to civil disorder, with Leeds (1925) and Birmingham (1926) somewhat surprisingly a little late in joining the trend. Even the large city of Glasgow did not establish a unit until 1924, so Bristol can justifiably claim to be a real pioneer amongst the provincial forces.

The Chief Constable of Bristol, Henry Allbutt, would not have been a stranger to the world of horses. He had been Deputy Chief Constable of the Liverpool Police before his appointment in Bristol in 1894, and would have seen the Mounted Branch in action in that city. He received £100 per annum to maintain his own horse for official purposes, and many of his duties involved the purchase and disposal of the animals. In the summer of 1899 he had to report to the Watch Committee that the horse *Jumbo* was having a problem in drawing the Prison Van, and a few weeks later he further reported that the same horse had bolted on 9th August while in charge of the small Prison Van in Broadmead. It was resolved that the horse be exchanged for another - no doubt to the relief of drivers and prisoners alike! In September of the same year (about the time the

Mounted Branch was formed) he received a request from his four Superintendents at Central, Redland, St. George and Bedminster for permission to acquire horse-drawn dog-carts so that they could "more efficiently superintend their districts".

Dealing with horses was a regular part of police life. All the stations were equipped with stable accommodation and the equipment necessary for the maintenance of the horses' welfare. In 1898, with the expansion of the city and consequent additional responsibilities of fire-fighting, the Brigade (part of the Police Force until 1941) was increased in strength by eight horses. Four of these went to St.George, two to Bedminster and two to Redland. Because of the requirements of the Fire Brigade, the stables at these stations would have been quite large, and the addition of nine police horses at the various locations appears not to have presented any difficulties.

Unfortunately records no longer exist which detail the selection of the first mounted officers or how the new Branch was distributed across the city, although it seems certain that all four Districts would have been stations for at least two members of the new unit. The fittest and most able constables would have been interviewed and selected for the job, and previous cavalry experience and competence on escort may well have been high on the list of requisite attributes. Since only the comparatively well-to-do owned their own horses, the job would have been considered prestigious enough to attract a good number of well-qualified officers.

The first officer in charge of the new unit was Inspector Turner. It was his responsibility to set up the Branch, and he would have been selected because of his relevant experience. With military service a common previous occupation in the Force, Inspector Turner may well have been a former cavalryman. Judging by the steady increase in the strength of the Branch over the next few years, he was obviously a competent man who had made out a good case for his unit.

The new group of mounted officers, with probably a large percentage of former cavalrymen amongst their ranks, turned quite naturally for advice to the body which had used horses for hundreds of years in all types of situations and with all types of equipment - the Army. The Bristol Constabulary Mounted Section adopted as their bible the British Army Cavalry Manual, and from it selected horses and equipment appropriate for use by the police. At this time the selection of horses (which later became the responsibility of the Section's Horsemaster) was delegated to a sub-committee of the Watch Committee, consisting of Alderman Dix and Mr Stephens. The names of these two gentlemen appear continuously in the minutes of meetings in connection with the acquisition and disposal of horses, and they must have been knowledgeable and expert in their field to undertake the work. For example, in July 1900 "the Chief Constable reported that the chestnut horse *Boston* was unfit for police purposes, and it was resolved that Alderman Dix and Mr. Stephens be authorised to sell the same for the best price they can obtain and to buy a new one". This stalwart pair continued the same sterling work for many years. The partnership ended in 1913 with the death of Alderman Dix, but Mr Stephens continued his service, later becoming an Alderman of the Council. He died in 1926.

The horses selected were those of a stamp favoured by the Army: half to three-quarter bred hunter-type geldings, at least 16 hands in height (a "hand" equals 4 inches and is measured from the withers to the base of the foreleg) with big bone and a solid conformation capable of carrying a fully grown man and all his equipment. The oldest surviving photographs show some good dependable-looking horses, suitable for the work the police required of them. Nervous, highly-strung or temperamental animals would have found no place in the police stables, subjected as they always have been to sights and sounds dimly, if ever, understood by the equine brain. The horses would have been capable of being trained to accept distractions and frights all around them, with the intention of utilising them in busy city streets and with the possibility of crowd control work. The initial selection process was a very important part of the job and Messrs Dix and Stephens had the experience to select the right type of animal from what would have been, at that time, an enormous market.

Uniform was established after a military pattern, but with blue serge replacing khaki. Basic requirements were approved at the Watch Committee meeting of September 1899 when tenders were also required to be obtained "from Mr Radford and Mr Wintle for the supply of Night and Day rugs for the horses". In March 1900 - after the winter! - it was "resolved that tenders for the supply of cloaks for the mounted police (be requested) from the present uniform contractors". In January 1902 further protective clothing was obtained when "the Chief Constable submitted quotations for nine pairs of leggings and spurs for the mounted men, and it was resolved that it be left to Alderman Sir Herbert Ashman and the Chief Constable to decide upon the pattern to be purchased".

Bridles, saddles and trappings were also after the military model, and the effectiveness of this choice can be judged by the fact that the equipment remains largely unchanged to the present day. The suppliers of saddles and trappings at the time were "Messrs. Shattock, Hunter and Co." The saddles adopted were those of the military officer, uncompromising in their comfort for the rider but having the advantage of being readily available and familiar to the newly appointed officers. The bridles, the main part of which was the head collar (for ease of securing horses while on the march with the Army), also incorporated the military bit (or universal reversible), a double-rein bit which assisted the rider in maintaining control over the animal even in the most trying circumstances.

The work required of the Mounted Branch in the very early days would have consisted of the employment briefly described by Henry Allbutt in his initial report. They were required to patrol the outer areas of their districts and other areas less accessible to men on foot, and to carry the many dispatches between headquarters at Central and the three distant stations. The full-time police horses would have made some impact on the streets, crowded as they were with horse-drawn vehicles of all descriptions. From the very start the height from the ground of the mounted policeman made him readily identifiable in a busy thoroughfare, and the advantages of the mounted patrols in relation to their accessibility to the public, and their deterrent effect upon wrong-doers, were quickly apparent. Parts of the Force which were at some distance from the police stations had previously received only fleeting visits from men on foot. Now they could receive the worthwhile attention of a high-profile patrolling officer. Thus the Mounted officers were in a real sense helping to fulfil the original object of the police service as laid down by Bristol's first Chief of Police, Joseph Bishop, in his Regulation Book of 1836. In it he stated that "*the principle object of the police establishment is the prevention of crime. To this great end every effort is to be directed: the public security of persons and property and the preservation of the public tranquillity and good order in the Borough will be better effected than by the detection and punishment of offenders after they have succeeded in violating the laws*".

This inspired vision, together with "the protection of life", remains the principle objective of the police service today.

Mounted Police escort in Clifton, c.1904

The new unit also gathered periodically to provide the mounted escort for the City's dignitaries on those formal occasions when they attended church services as a body, or at the opening of the Quarter Sessions or Assizes. They would have been aware that the disreputable condition of previous escorts had led in part to the formation of the full-time Mounted Branch, and were determined that no such criticism could be levelled at them. There is no doubt that the eyes of the City Council would have been upon them during those first few escorts to ensure that their investment in safeguarding civic dignity was being rewarded. They would not have been disappointed. The mounted escort then set a standard which has been maintained across the century; and one hundred years later this historic function is continued by the current Mounted Section, with modern counterparts taking as much pride as their forebears in their appearance and bearing, which add so much to the dignity of the occasion.

The Watch Committee minutes refer to some of the names applied to the police horses in the first few years of the Branch. In addition to *Boston* referred to earlier, the following names are recorded:

In June 1903, after advice from the Veterinary Surgeon, the bay horses *Prince* and *Sancho* were replaced by two new purchases and the same happened to *Billy*, three months later. The following year, a bay horse *Bosun* was sold for £310, and a new horse purchased for an additional £340. In 1906 the committee discussed the bay horse *Coronation* (purchased in 1902 perhaps?) which required to be blistered and turned out to grass for a month. In 1907 the Veterinary Surgeon submitted a report to the Watch Committee to the effect that he had examined the bay horse *Tommy* and found that *"his fore-fetlocks and elbow joints were slightly swollen. It was resolved that the horse be turned out to grass for a month as recommended"*. The treatment must have been successful, because *Tommy* appears again in a report dated October 1910. Then it was reported that "the Chief Constable has drawn attention to the fact that the horses *Major* and *Tommy* which were purchased in 1899 for police purposes, and now aged 16 years, are not fit for the work required of them. The horses should be disposed of and Alderman Dix and Mr Stephens be requested to purchase two new horses".

The strength of the Mounted Branch remained at nine (one officer and eight men) until 1904, when the establishment was increased to 12. The purchase of additional horses and equipment was voted through, and on 12th July 1904 it was "resolved that 12 new cavalry swords with scabbards be obtained for the mounted police". These would have been used for ceremonial purposes.

The Chief Constable responsible for the founding of the unit, Henry Allbutt, was dismissed from the service in September 1906, under somewhat mysterious circumstances. He had been a dynamic and forthright officer, and had been responsible for many innovations and developments which improved the efficiency of the Force and the welfare of the personnel. An auction was made of the former Chief Constable's furniture and effects, and this attempt to raise money could indicate that Henry Allbutt had somehow got himself into debt, an offence punishable in the

James Cann

police force of the time with instant dismissal. James Cann was appointed in his place. He was not a Bristolian, but had served in the Bristol force through all ranks from constable. He was a very popular figure, and his appointment was welcomed on all sides.

The reputation of the effectiveness of the Mounted Branch had spread to the surrounding forces within a few years of its inception, and requests from the neighbouring Chief Constables for permission to employ them in their own areas were being received at Bristol's headquarters. These requests required the permission of the Watch Committee before approval, and in April 1907 the Committee "read a letter from the Chief Constable of Newport, Monmouthshire, asking whether the Committee would be prepared to supply six mounted constables for one week, in the event of their requiring such assistance on the occasion of the visit of the Prince of Wales to Newport in June next". Approval was granted.

In May 1908 the Chief Constable was authorised to obtain 4 sets of saddlery, and also "to have the old dress uniform of the Inspector touched up". This slightly odd instruction may have been because that at about this time the Committee received a letter from the Chief Constable of Bath asking for the services of eight mounted men and an officer to perform an escort on the occasion of the visit of the American Ambassador (the Hon. Whitelaw Reid) to Bath on 22nd October. It was resolved that the request be complied with, subject to the payment of the expenses incurred.

Bristol Mounted Police escorting the American Ambassador in Milsom St, Bath, Oct 1908

But it was in situations of public disorder that the mounted unit really proved its worth. The years leading up to the First World War were marked by an upsurge in industrial unrest, as union membership became more organised among working men. New tactics such as demonstrations, marches and picket lines were most unsettling to the authorities, and the police were again used to prevent and sometimes suppress any resultant disorder.

The collieries in Somerset were, like their counterparts in South Wales, particularly subject to demonstrations and disruptions as the unions attempted to improve the miserable lot of the workforce. In January 1909 the Chief Constable reported that he had received a request from the Chief Constable of Somerset for the assistance of 6 mounted police "in consequence of some rioting which had taken place near Radstock", and that he had acceded to the request. During the spring of the same year the Chief Constable of Somerset again requested that mounted officers be sent to Dunkerton Colliery, just outside Bath. The effectiveness of their presence later led to a letter of appreciation from the Somerset Standing Joint Committee "expressing their thanks for the promptness in lending the mounted constables to assist during the recent disturbances at Dunkerton Colliery". The following summer the unit dealt with disturbances at Wincanton, having had their expenses paid as usual. The repeated requests from Somerset, and the following year from the South Wales coalfields, demonstrated how necessary the services of the Mounted Branch had become.

Somerset miners were happy to pose with the Bristol police horses! c.1909

Apart from the Mounted Branch's own growing reputation, the regular requests for aid from the neighbouring forces partly stemmed from a Home Office Circular dated 15th April 1909. This was drafted in an effort to provide guidelines for the police in the face of growing union organisation, and was entitled *"Employment of the Military in aid of the Police"*. In it the Home Secretary, referring to the lack of organisation in mutual assistance between Forces, bemoaned the fact that *"so little advantage has been taken of the means to that end, provided by Section 25 of the Police Act 1890"*. Under the subtitle *"Mounted Police"*, the Circular goes on:

"The Select Committee also expressed the opinion that the maintenance of mounted police is very desirable and that, in addition to a permanent mounted force, provision might be made for special emergencies by the temporary employment as mounted men of any police officers serving in the force who possess experience of cavalry or yeomanry work. The value of mounted police in both dealing with actual rioters and in breaking up a crowd which, if left to itself, might become tumultuous, is recognised by all those who have had to deal with disorderly crowds, and the desirability of maintaining such a force as a precautionary measure is a point which His Majesty's Inspectors of Constabulary have constantly kept in view..."

This forthright encouragement for mounted units from the Home Office must have been gratifying for the Bristol Constabulary and its Mounted Branch but, as we have seen, did not lead to a rush of forces to comply with the recommendation for their more widespread institution. Moreover, it did not result in the Bristol Watch Committee acceding to the suggestion that it enter into Standing Agreements with other Forces to supply aid. All requests for such agreements were turned down in the same terms: "Regret we cannot see our way to enter into a standing agreement but would be prepared to give any assistance in our power in case of an emergency". This stance at least left the discretion and authority to supply aid in the hands of the Watch Committee without being bound by any Standing Agreement which may later have proved inappropriate.

In June 1909, encouraged by the success and popularity of the young Mounted Branch and with the support of the Home Office, the Watch Committee "resolved that the number of Mounted Police be increased by 12 constables to be selected from the Force, and that the Chief Constable be authorised to obtain 12 sets of

Superintendent William Macey

harness and equipment at an estimated cost of £132 and to make arrangements for obtaining the necessary number of horses". This brought the strength of the unit up to 24 officers and horses. At a meeting in November 1909 the Chief Constable reported that 25 pairs of new jackboots were required for the Mounted Police, and he was authorised to obtain such boots. This expansion would have involved the Watch Committee in considerable expense, but with the prevailing atmosphere of unrest, they apparently felt it to be money well spent.

The Inspector in charge of the Branch at this time was William Thomas Macey. He was a strict disciplinarian, but was also regarded as being fair. He supervised the Branch until the temporary dissolution caused by the First World War, and was later promoted to Superintendent in charge of the Redland Division.

He led several mounted escorts in this capacity, and the photograph dating from 1919 shows him leading a ceremonial march-past outside the Royal West of England Academy while the Lord Mayor acknowledges the salute. It was while he was in Redland Police Station in 1923 preparing for another such parade that he collapsed and died at the early age of 55. His cortége was accorded the honour of a full ceremonial police escort, one of the last occasions that such an impressive parade was mounted for a deceased member.

During the summer of 1910, the industrial unrest came closer to home with a strike of dock labourers at the port of Avonmouth, and the horses were again employed in containing civil disorder, which had occurred as a result. This was a more violent occasion, and on 20th July the Chief Constable had to report that "two horses belonging to the Force had been injured in a conflict with the strikers at Avonmouth". There were claims and counter-claims of violence on both sides, and the Bristol Strikes Council and the Bristol Disputes Council wrote letters to the Committee asking that an Inquiry be held with reference to the action of the police during the strike. Perhaps unsurprisingly, no evidence was forthcoming that any person was

Superintendent Macey leading a mounted parade in 1919

injured in consequence of the police action, and so the case for an Inquiry was dropped. The Committee then unanimously approved the action of the police during the strike and made a note that the work had been performed with great credit to the Force.

Between these skirmishes of industrial unrest, the horses and men of the Mounted Branch continued their patrols of the city and its districts. The unit, now with ten years' experience behind them, had become a familiar sight on the streets of Bristol and, in addition to ordinary patrols and dispatch-carrying, were also used to direct the motorised vehicular traffic which was becoming much more evident. The strength of the Branch remained at 24 until 1912, when the Government Inspector, still demonstrating official approval of such units, recommended that the Watch Committee "should establish a permanent Mounted Force for the purpose of patrolling the outlying districts of the city". This recommendation, it appears, must have come about as a result of the ever-widening boundaries of the city and consequent inability of the local Force, even with its horses, to police it adequately. By the summer of 1912 the Mounted Branch had attained its greatest strength of 31 which, with the onrush of the first Great War, was soon to be greatly reduced. It never recovered such heights again.

CC James Cann and his superintendents pose with the officers of the Bristol Constabulary Mounted Section, c.1912

1914 - 1920

The Mounted Section reached its greatest numerical strength just before the onset of the First World War, and it is not difficult to understand why this was so. The horse was still the most favoured form of transport, if only for its familiarity and its comparative cost to buy and run, as opposed to the motor-car. But the commercial use of the horse was in the very twilight of its years, and as the century progressed those who maintained their horse vehicles in the face of the increasingly efficient and cheaper alternative of the motor car became fewer and fewer.

Trooper William Bishop in the uniform of the 1st Life Guards

Pre-war industrial unrest was a major factor in deciding the strength of the Mounted Section at this time and, with the local Watch Committee obviously concerned to control any disturbances in their area, they must have considered that the unit was indispensable in helping to maintain the peace, even without the encouragement of the Home Office. No-one could foresee the convulsion and rapid acceleration in technology which the War would bring, and which would render inappropriate both the expense and the need for such a large contingent of police horses. Communication between police stations was now improving beyond measure by the telephone and motor vehicle, thereby making the policing of the whole

Force area more efficient. This removed from the Mounted Section two of the principle reasons for its existence in such numbers. However in the short term it was not the removal of basic tasks which eroded the Mounted Section, but the loss of men to the war.

On the day war was declared - 4th August 1914 - the strength of the Bristol Constabulary stood at 617 men. No less than 266 of these left during the course of the next few months and years to join the Army or Navy, and, as the *Historical Review of the Bristol Constabulary 1836-1934* recorded: *"Every man was a volunteer - they did not have to be compelled by force of law to serve their country in its need. By definition the men who left for the war were the youngest, the fittest and the most spirited. Of these the best found their way to the fighting regiments. In their lonely graves lie the best of a generation."*

PC Bishop at Bedminster Police Station, 1908

Many officers of the Mounted Branch had come from a military background, and were amongst the first to rejoin the colours. One such was PC 157A William Alfred Bishop, known as "Nobby". He was born at Bitton in 1880, and like many of his generation joined the British Army, ending up as a Trooper in the 1st Life Guards. He saw active service in South Africa during the Boer War and finally left the Army after 5 years 60 days service. He joined the Bristol Constabulary on 11th December 1907 and in keeping with his cavalry background, soon became a member of the Mounted Branch. The marvellous photograph of him was taken in 1908. He poses proudly on his fine bay horse in the yard at the Bedminster stables, complete with rolled mac, cross belt and pill-box cap, with naked sword at the slope. A mounted officer of today would recognise any of the equipment (except for the cap) and his breeches display a surprisingly modern cut. Evidently the large wings, so fashionable on later types of breeches and jodhpurs, had yet to put in an appearance. It is tragic that his story is known mainly because he became the first Bristol policeman to be killed in the First World War. He died of wounds received at the first battle of Ypres, on the 22nd October 1914, and was buried in the nearby town cemetery, a distinction not afforded to so many who fell in the later months and years of the War. He left a young widow and two-year-old son, Ernest Alfred.

On 2nd December 1914 the Chief Constable informed the Watch Committee of the loss, the first of many such reports. The Committee resolved to pay the widow the sum she was receiving while her husband was serving with the colours, "until the Town Clerk is in a position to report what amount the Committee should pay to the dependants". This apparently did not amount to much. His widow was unable to cope with the demands of her young family, and Ernest was subsequently placed in the Bristol Constabulary orphanage in Cotham Park. He remained there until rejoining his family at Aldershot ten years later.*

James Cann had resigned as Chief Constable in September 1914 because of ill health, and he died a few months later. John Henderson Watson, who was to be the first Chief Constable to be provided with a motor car, replaced him. The old horse-drawn steam Fire Engine, which had been the pride of the Force in 1877 (so much so that it had been exhibited at the Zoo!) was also pensioned off at this time, to be replaced by a new motor turbine Fire Engine. The modern world was catching up with the Bristol Constabulary, and its horses were becoming redundant.

In January 1915, only five months after the outbreak of war, the War Office requested "one or more" mounted officers from Bristol to be enlisted as army recruits - an astonishingly modest request in the light of the subsequent millions engulfed by the War. However, Watson regarded his force as being already seriously depleted and was forced to turn down the request.

*NOTE I was privileged to meet the 83-year-old Ernest and his daughter Linda Pitts when they visited the police stables at Bower Ashton in 1995. I am grateful for their help in providing details of William Bishop's history and for their permission to use the two photographs.

In April four horses were publicly auctioned off at a loss. A further six horses were soon afterwards sold for £424.4s.0d, compared with the price paid by the   Committee of £320.

The Mounted Branch had already given their all to the War effort, and for the duration the unit ceased to exist. From the Chief Constable's post-war efforts to reform the Branch it is apparent that most, if not all, of the horses had either been sold or donated to the Government.

The Great War dragged on to its third and fourth year and, of the 266 men who had volunteered from the Bristol Force, 110 were destined to be killed or injured, a staggering 41.3%. It was hardly surprising that several innovations were employed to make up the shortfall in manpower caused by the War, and amongst these were the use of Specials (who evolved from the Police Reserve set up in 1911), the employment of police women (although attestation as constable had to wait until 1931), and the retaining of police officers who were about to retire.

The use of women in what had been an exclusively male preserve was initially regarded with ridicule by the public, and a male constable was always required to escort his female colleague around the town, for the sake of decorum and to protect her against possible attack. However after the War the mockery gave way to much ill-feeling as the men returned to find their jobs usurped by women. Nevertheless in this area too, the Bristol Constabulary were pioneers as women became increasingly involved with the work of the Force. It is interesting to note however that the Mounted Section was to remain an exclusively male preserve until as late as 1980! When the war ended in November 1918, the world had changed forever. Soldiers and sailors returned home to find that their jobs had either disappeared or had been taken over by cheaper labour. Police grievances included the fact that pensions had not kept pace with the increase in the

John Henderson Watson

cost of living, and some men who had been wounded in the armed forces were liable to be rejected on their return through being "physically incapable of undertaking the duties of a police constable".

However, the main cause for complaint was pay, compared with pre-war levels. The demands of the war had pushed the provision of essential services and supplies up to a much higher priority, and the consequent rise in wages left the police pay levels far behind. In 1919, a constable with 20 years service was earning £2.10s.0d a week, compared with a carter who received £3.8s.0d per week. Social upheaval caused by mass unemployment was looming, and it became vital to restore the attractiveness of the police service as a career. The Police Act of 1919 was formulated as a result of the Desborough Committee (set up to examine the pay and conditions of police forces nationally) and allowed for the formation of a union known as the Police Federation. Police pay was standardised and increased to £3.10s.0d per week on joining, rising to £4.15s.0d.

In Bristol, Chief Constable John Watson was authorised by the Watch Committee to buy eighteen horses for the Mounted Branch. By March 1919 John Watson reported that "he had purchased 12 horses for the use of the mounted police at a cost of £356.7s.0d". Eleven horses were purchased at Wrexham Auction Mart and one at Hereford Auction. The following month he reported that he had purchased an additional six horses at Shirehampton for Mounted Police work at a total cost of £230, making a total spent of £586.7s.0d. Although at just over half its pre-war strength, the Mounted Branch was once again a going concern. Mounted police were again able to patrol the outlying areas of Bristol and assisted in the busy city streets, unaware that a cloud of disapproval was about to burst upon their heads.

The reinstatement of the Mounted Section inevitably involved the expenditure of a not inconsiderable amount of money, and this did not go unchallenged. The emerging Labour Party had changed the balance of power in the Council Chamber, and there were some strident objections to the reinstatement of the Branch. There were bitter memories of the Mounted Section being used before the War in reducing the impact of Union-sponsored industrial strikes, and the prospect of uniformed and jack-booted mounted officers being employed in a similar capacity after the war seemed too much to stomach.

In a Council meeting on 20th January 1920, Councillor Perrett demanded to know the number and annual cost of the Mounted Police and Police Women respectively; and when the Chairman had furnished the information, he moved that the Watch Committee be requested to consider the desirability of dispensing with or greatly reducing the number of Mounted Police and Police Women. In the absence of a quorum the motion was not proceeded with at the time, but the following month the motion was put before the Council again. A local newspaper report dated 10th February 1920 gave a full account of the discussion concerning the issue, which illuminated the attitude of the various members towards the Mounted Branch. The report was as follows:

Mr C.R.Perrett moved that the Watch Committee be requested to consider the desirability of dispensing with, or greatly reducing, the number of Mounted Police and Police Women. He said that many people complained that money was being wasted upon those sections of the police force. If Police Women were necessary they should be of mature years. The present women police were a laughing stock. (Laughter) The 12 women police cost £1574, and the 18 Mounted Police cost £6800. The latter paraded the streets but did very little. One of their uses was to take the Lord Mayor to church, and he agreed with that. (Laughter) He urged that the rates should be kept down, and he added that although Alderman Swaish (the Chairman of the Watch Committee) said that the Government paid half the cost, the money had to be paid by taxpayers. (Hear, hear!)

The Revd Jarman seconded, as a matter of form, and urged the importance of economy. Mr Burgess defended women police but objected to Mounted Police. He asserted that the presence of Mounted Police in the streets had not a peaceful influence. Although they had maligned Prussianism there was still a sneaking regard for it, and the Mounted Police were a tin-pot exhibition of it. He proposed that the women police should be omitted from the resolution, and Mr Senington seconded as a member of the Watch Committee, remarking that he did not think they needed Mounted Police for the Lord Mayor or the Assize Judges. Mr Thompson asserted that Birmingham had decided against Mounted Police, but the Home Secretary had ruled against them. By whom was Bristol to be ruled, by that Council, or by the Home Secretary? Mr Witty said that law and order had to be maintained and the

Home Secretary would have a larger view of the question. Alderman Whitefield having advocated the retention of women police, Mr Perrett said he would withdraw them from his proposal.

Mr Pearce stated that the object of the Government was to frighten (No!) or deter people from creating local trouble. It was a step in the wrong direction. The presence of Mounted Police created a bad atmosphere. He was a peaceful man, but they had almost made him an anarchist. (Laughter) A general feeling of hatred was growing up against the police force. (No! and True!) He hoped Municipal Authorities would bring pressure to bear on the Home Office. Mr Gane deprecated suggestions as to ulterior motives. He added that Bolshevism was a force in this country today, and the Labour members must know that the wise leaders of the Trades Unions encouraged the Government to maintain the police as a barrier and for the preservation of law and order, which was in the best interests of the working classes. He reminded the Council that Mounted Police in Bristol were not new, and asked "Why that attitude of suspicion?" Alderman Whitefield replied: "Because of the increase." Mr Gane added that there had only been an increase from 12 to 18. He urged that they should all cultivate mutual confidence.

Mr Ayles characterised Mr Gane's speech as a most unfortunate one. He maintained that the large increase in Special Constables and Mounted Police was made as a result of the labour troubles 1911-1912. The best way to avoid violence, he urged, was to do away with displays that provoked violence. He suggested that they should substitute bicycles for horses in the outlying districts. The resolution as amended was adopted".

The following day the Town Clerk informed the Watch Committee that the Council had passed the resolution that they be requested to consider the desirability of dispensing with or greatly reducing the number of Mounted Police. In the absence of the Chief Constable it was resolved that consideration of the matter be deferred. For the first but certainly not the last time this century, the Mounted Police were having to fight for their very existence.

CHAPTER FOUR

THE INTER-WAR YEARS

In March 1920 the Chief Constable found himself under pressure to justify the expense, duties and current strength (18 horses and officers) of the Mounted Branch to the Watch Committee. The Chief Constable, who had after all reformed the unit, was obviously convinced of its value in the light of the continuing industrial and social unrest, and with Home Office encouragement he managed to reassure the Watch Committee, and eventually the Council. From now on, however, there would always be voices raised in opposition to the unit, arguing that the expense was not justified because it was anachronistic in the modern world of motor vehicles and ever-improving communications.

The principle role of the Mounted Police at this time was little changed from its inception, except that they were no longer required to "carry the mail" to and from police stations. They were still to be seen on regular district patrols, covering the areas that were too far distant for the foot officers, and were also maintained to assist wherever police were required to supervise large crowds. The ceremonial escort was still a regular feature of Mounted Branch life and civic enthusiasm for the continuance of this duty remained undiminished. In addition to the more usual mayoral escorts, 1921 saw the institution of the Annual Memorial Police Church Parade held in memory of comrades who had fallen in the Great War. The Mounted Branch naturally played a full part in the Parade and ceremony of the event, the culmination of which was Divine Service in either Bristol Cathedral or Broadmead Chapel.

One duty that had become the norm for the mounted officers before the War was now removed: that of the specific control of motorised traffic in the city. The move foresaw the shape of things to come. In 1925 motor vehicles were placed upon the roads of the country at the rate of at least 500,000 per annum, and a report stated that "policemen engaged in controlling traffic must be men of iron constitution and sound nervous system"! The Chief Constable's decision pre-empted any problem that may have arisen as a result of placing the police horses in this unenviable position.

The Watch Committee's reports on the subject of police horses were cutting no ice in some quarters of the City Council. On 8th June 1920 Councillor Perrett enquired "what action was the Watch Committee taking generally in regard to women police and Mounted Police with a view to reducing expense. He had had many complaints as to the expense of this item". Although the Watch Committee was able to defuse this particular onslaught, by early 1921 the Chief Constable decided to respond to the continuing criticism. The Branch was reduced from 18 to 14 officers and horses, the number he considered the minimum for the duties envisaged for them and which he had outlined in his earlier report.

The reduction in horses was partially achieved by natural wastage, with horses no longer fit for police work not being replaced. In March 1921 police horse *Patsy* was certified by the Veterinary Surgeon to be suffering from a tumour and chronic abscess in the abdomen, and was accordingly taken to the Zoological Gardens and destroyed. It is recorded that the sum of £2.2s.0d was received for the carcass and skin. The same month the Chief Constable disposed of two horses from the Central station, and he was required by the Committee "to communicate with the local farmers as to whether they would purchase same". In June he reported that police horses *Sancho* and *Peter*, aged 23 and 18 respectively, could now be disposed of, and recommended that they be sent to the Zoo. He further reported that horses *Met* and *Satan* had developed bad tempers and were unsafe to ride in traffic, and recommended that they be sold by auction and replaced. An amusing report was given concerning the police horse *Magic* which continually injured itself through falling down whilst asleep! In this case it was recommended that the horse be turned out to grass for the remainder of the summer and, if not then cured of the habit, to be sold and replaced. *Magic* was cured by the treatment and went on to give several more years of good service, presumably managing to stay awake when on duty!

The Horsemaster (the officer in charge of the Mounted Branch) was at this time Sergeant Bees, who was stationed at Central. The rank of Inspector had been removed from the group following the reduction in size when the Branch had been reinstated after the War. The stables at Central were just off the main yard, and Sgt. Bees office was above the stables and next to the Harness Room. He remained in the supervisory position (although joined by Sergeant Thomas Parker in 1925 when the Branch was again increased to 21) until his retirement in 1934.

In July 1922 the Chief Constable received a letter from the Officer Commanding 4th Gloucestershire Regiment, calling attention to the difficulty of obtaining suitable horses for the use of officers at the Battalion Parade, and asking whether on these occasions the Watch Committee would allow him the use of the police horses. The application was acceded to, subject to the horses being insured while so used. The request seems to demonstrate how quickly the Army had cast its horses since the turn of the century.

Sir John Swaish

In September of the same year, one dozen horse sheets were purchased from Messrs Shattock and Hunter at 19s each. This firm had been dealing with the Mounted Branch from the very beginning, and they must have been grateful for the patronage in an age that witnessed the almost total eclipse of the working horse. During the same month Councillor Perrett (obviously not one to be put off!) again raised the question as to the cost of women police and Mounted Police, and whether the Watch Committee intended to retain them. Sir John Swaish replied that he had only recently answered a similar question. For the year ending last March (1921-1922) "the cost of the women police was £1753 and the Mounted Police cost £3100 for 14 mounted men. The numbers had been reduced as far as efficiency would permit". One gets the feeling that Sir John was beginning to regard Mr Perrett's questions on the subject as a trifle wearisome! In fact Mr Perrett was still objecting to women police in September of the following year, when he also complained that there were 30 women in the Docks Office and 16 in the Electrical Office, and they were drawing £3 or £4 per week. "Let them go to service," Councillor Perrett urged, "and replace them by men who are walking about the streets and cannot get work." Mr Perrett's views were by no means unusual, or indeed particularly controversial, in that time of the post-war Depression.

In June 1923 Sir John Swaish, in answer to questions from Councillor Parker, stated that "four motor-cars had been purchased for the use of the police superintendents in Bristol. One cost £195, and three cost £200 each. (What was the difference for £5, one wonders today?) The estimated upkeep per annum was £200 for the four. The horses that were used by the superintendents were transferred to the Mounted Branch to replace horses that had been disposed of as being no longer fit for mounted work. The superintendents' carriages have been sold". This would indicate that the superintendents had been using their dog-carts, obtained in 1899, until as late as 1923 - nine years after the Chief Constable had been provided with his motor-car!

The Mounted Section was still stabled at the four main stations in the city - Central, Redland, Bedminster and St.George, although use was made of other locations, including Fishponds and Horfield. In his excellent book *"Policing Bristol"* Michael Osborne briefly describes how the flat above Fishponds Police Station was inhabited for a time by a mounted officer and his wife. The good lady was expected to act as matron in the station, supply food for the prisoners and be on call if a female was arrested! (This use of policemen's wives in such situations was also a feature of life at Redland for many years.) The mounted officer at Fishponds also "groomed the cob which drew the Superintendent's gig as well as his own horse and at 8.15 each morning he drove the Superintendent to Divisional Headquarters at St.George".

The officers continued to patrol their own districts and assembled for ceremonial escorts, parades, inspections or police operations. The photograph shows PC 79D Tom Palmer, who was sta-

PC Palmer on Victor, St George Police Station 1924

tioned at St.George between 1924 and 1927, preparing to leave the yard at that station on police horse *Victor*. Tom is wearing his cloak in anticipation of a cold patrol! *Victor* was, according to Tom's widow Hilda, one of the Chief Constable's favourite horses, and looking at him it is not difficult to see why.

About this time additional duties were being allocated to the Mounted Section which supplemented their patrols in the outlying districts of the Force, and replaced some of the duties removed by social and police modernisation. It had always been accepted that the high-profile nature of mounted police patrols was beneficial in preventing some types of crime and anti-social behaviour. Consequently, in about the mid-1920s, specific mounted patrols of the Downs area of Bristol were instituted following complaints that "interference of young ladies (was taking place) upon the Downs, and also wanton damage was being caused to certain seats on the Downs". The Chief Constable later filed a report in answer to the complaints, in which he stated: "The supervision of the Downs by ordinary uniformed and plain clothes patrols has been materially increased during the past two or three years by the addition of mounted and cycle patrols. The mounted patrols have proved very effective, inasmuch as they are able to cover more ground and patrol secluded parts of the Downs". From this time, in an effort to prevent the type of offence prevalent in such areas, the specific duty of patrol of the grassed areas of Durdham Downs has become one of the more pleasant duties of the mounted officer.

The continuing social unrest was soon to bring more than preventative work for the Mounted Branch. There were sporadic minor outbreaks of disorder relating to industrial disputes, and demonstrations and marches complaining about the high levels of unemployment, culminating in the General Strike of May 1926. Generally these passed off peacefully, but occasionally disorder would ensue. One such incident was witnessed by young Graham Fowler in Old Market in the summer of 1926. He had just been taken on by the large Soap Works in Broad Plain and part of his duties consisted in running errands into the centre of town to distribute or collect items for the Works. As he was leaving the factory a large group of demonstrators, whom he believed to be the East Bristol Miners, were congregating in Old Market; and when he returned by way of Castle Street a full scale riot was in progress, with police officers on foot attempting but failing to maintain order. Graham Fowler remembers seeing two trams at one end of Lower Castle Street near the junction with Old Market and, as he watched, a mounted contingent comprising possibly 12 horses and men moved out from between the two trams and turned into Old Market. The Mounted officers formed a double line and advanced "at speed" towards the crowd. Mr Fowler described it as "sweeping the street" and said that within minutes the crowd had dispersed down the side streets and did not reassemble. He was able to return to work via Old Market and nearly 70 years later was able to relate to me the view and impressions he had on that day, which he said appeared to be a very effective and efficient operation by the police. This was indeed one of the operations involving police horses that remained in the Section's memory, and was repeated (with variations) along with other similar incidents to all new recruits to the unit, including the present author! Mr Graham Fowler introduced himself to me after I had given a talk to a group of which he was a member, and it was a great bonus to have an actual eye-witness account of an incident which had become shrouded in Mounted mythology!

The Mounted Branch in the mid-to-late '20's appeared to be earning their keep and the replacement of horses lost through various ailments presented no problem for the Watch Committee. Expenditure for 1925-1926 included the sum of £1500 for "horses, harness and forage". Dissent from the Council had also been muted, due to the increase in civil disorders, and the strength of the Branch was once again increased by 7 horses to a total of 21 horses and men.

In January 1926 a letter was received by the Watch Committee from the Secretary of the Southern Command Horse Show at Tidworth in Wiltshire calling attention to the fact that "at the last two Horse Shows, entries were invited from Police Authorities in respect of the Mounted Police Class, but very little support had been forthcoming". He asked whether in the event of a similar class being provided at the next Show the Bristol Watch Committee would permit any of the mounted police to enter. It was cautiously resolved (Alderman Robinson dissenting) that "as an experiment the Committee are prepared to sanction two entries from the Bristol Mounted Police". It was argued from the start that the training for, and competition in, horse shows could only bring benefit to the Section in its regular work, and so it proved. On 11th August 1926 the Chief Constable was able to report to a gratified Committee that the two horses shown in the Tidworth Show gained 1st and 2nd prize, and he also informed them that he had a balance of £15 representing the prize money received in connection with the Show. He recommended that the money should be retained for the purpose of paying the entrance fees in the event of the Committee deciding to send any horses to future Shows, and it was resolved that the recommendation be adopted. Thus began a proud chapter in the history of Bristol's Mounted Section.

John Watson must have believed in striking while the iron was hot, because early in 1927 he reported that he had received a letter from Colonel P.R.Laurie, "one of the Chief Constables of the Metropolitan Police", asking that the Mounted Police in Bristol should be allowed to enter the competition for Mounted Police to be held at the forthcoming Horse Show at Imber Court. He was authorised to allow two men and horses to be entered. But the authorities at Imber were due to be disappointed that year. At a later meeting, the Chief Constable asked for authority to withdraw the entry and to send the two Mounted men to the Horse Show in connection with the Southern Command, which was to be held on the same date. He obviously believed in remaining loyal to the Show which had provided him with such success the previous year! It was resolved that the necessary sanction be given.

Mounted Branch inspection, 1927

The annual physical Inspection of the Force, which was a regular feature of police life up until the early 1960s, was held on 10th May 1927 when the inspecting officer was Sir Leonard Dunning, His Majesty's Inspector of Constabulary for the Southern District. The photograph shows him accompanied by John Watson, resplendent in his ceremonial uniform, inspecting the Mounted Section on Durdham Downs. The report given that year was "satisfactory". Later the seventh Annual Police Church Parade was held in memory for comrades who fell in the Great War.

Church Parade to Bristol Cathedral, 1928

In spite of the fact that only two horses and men had been authorised to compete at the Southern Command Horse Show at Tidworth, the records show that in fact five members attended. They are listed as: Constable Ernest Bradford 34A riding police horse *Duke*, Constable Leonard Hopkinson 112C riding police horse *Victor*, Constable William Kemp 116C riding police horse *Patsy*, Constable George Hill 123C riding police horse *James* and Constable Wilfred Shore 33D riding police horse *Paddy*.

Once again the Force was successful. PC Hopkinson on *Victor* was awarded the 1st prize, and PC Kemp on *Patsy* the 2nd prize; whilst

PC Hill on *James* was placed 4th. If any comment was made about the numbers involved, no record remains and was more than likely lost in the congratulations. The following year the Bristol Constabulary was equally successful at the Show, when PC Hopkinson riding *Kildare* was placed

Mounted escort in Clifton, 1929

1st; PC Kemp on *Victor* was 2nd; and PC Bradford on *Leinster* was 3rd. The Branch was laying a solid foundation for good equestrianism, but setbacks to their showfield ambitions were to develop in the near future.

Other horses appeared in the Watch Committee minutes for less happy reasons. In 1928 *Major* was certified unfit for police duty in consequence of ringbone, and he was sent off to the Zoo for slaughter, as was the custom. In 1929 police horse *Shamrock* was reported as suffering from capped elbows for the past four years, the only remedy being an operation which would probably leave unsightly scar marks rendering the animal unfit for Mounted police work. He was sold and replaced. Later the same year the Chief Constable reported that the police horse *Greyleg*, which had been purchased in January from Mr James of Totterdown, had become unmanageable when in the streets. He stated that Mr James was willing to replace it by another horse of equal original value, and the offer was accepted.

In 1928 an officer joined the Mounted Branch who was destined to lead it through the following three decades. Percy Smith, who was born in London in 1904, enlisted in the Royal Horse Guards (the Blues) in 1919, and left the colours

Trooper Percy Smith in the uniform of the Royal Horse Guards, 1927

in 1927 with the report: "Exemplary. An exceptionally good man. Honest and trustworthy". The same year he joined the Bristol Constabulary and soon became a member of the Mounted Section, stationed at Redland. When Sgt Bees retired in 1934 he was promoted to take his place, and on

Sgt Thomas Parker leads the charge!

the retirement of Sgt Parker in the following year, Percy Smith found himself in sole charge of the Branch as the Horsemaster.

The Mounted Section turned out in force once again for the 1929 Annual Inspection, which took place on the Downs. Following the event, the unit was photographed cantering away across the grass, led by Sergeant Thomas Joseph Parker. Tom Parker, who four years earlier had joined Sgt Bees as a Mounted supervisor, was stationed at Bedminster, and his daughter Meta wrote to me describing how she would visit the stables on a Sunday to watch her father grooming his beloved horse. "Then being invited into the adjoining Fireman's cottage which was smelling of Sunday dinner cooking, for lemonade and a cake warm from the oven. It was always a red-letter day when Pa led the Mounted Police in ceremonial uniform complete with swords, the ornate Lord Mayor's coach and Councillors with their posies through town to St.Mary Redcliffe Church on Rush Sunday. The beautiful, well-trained horses lined up opposite the North Door for the return

PC Hucker on Bridewell, Redland 1929

journey; what an exciting day that was! To me, my father Tom Parker was a knight in shining armour. I was so proud of him...". Sgt Parker retired in 1935. He served in the Home Guard during the Second World War and died in 1952.

As the 1920s gave way to the 1930s, the Mounted Section continued to attend the Tidworth and Imber Court Horse Shows with greater or lesser degrees of success, and in 1929 four officers and horses were entered for the Mounted Police Class of the International Horse Show at Olympia. At this show PC 129C Fred Hucker on police horse *Bridewell* was awarded 3rd prize, and the fine photograph of them was taken soon after the event at the entrance to Redland Police Station.

Once again, voices were heard in the Council chamber objecting to the size and cost of the unit. On 25th February 1930 Councillor Light moved a reduction of the Watch Committee's budget estimate by £2000. He felt the citizens would be solidly behind them if they dispensed with the horses of mounted police. He felt that the citizens resented the horses being on the roads today. They were a nuisance to traffic. Alderman Senington in reply said that he was sorry these matters had been raised in the absence of Sir John Swaish (who was seriously ill in February and March) but he could enlighten them on some points. The matter of horses was of old standing. They were used almost entirely in the outskirts of the city. There the subject rested for that day, but was raised again the following month.

Charles George Maby

March 1930 was to prove a momentous time for the Branch. The Chief Constable who had supported them for so long, John Henderson Watson, resigned his post amid rumours of irregularities regarding a house and garage in Stoke Bishop, and the use of fire constables in work on the buildings. The former Chief Constable was required to pay back £1559 over the incident, and the Watch Committee's minutes note that this amount had not been paid by September. John Watson died by his own hand in October, broken by the sad end to what had been a distinguished career. He was succeeded in July 1930 by Charles George Maby who had been Acting Chief Constable since March. Charles Maby was Bristol-born and had joined the Bristol Constabulary as a constable in 1908. He served in all ranks and prior to his appointment had been a Superintendent in charge of administration.

Charles Maby's first dealings with the Watch Committee did not seem to augur well for the Mounted Branch. On 12th March 1930 the minutes record that "the Acting Chief Constable reported that it had been the practice for horses from the Mounted Police to be entered for certain horse shows and asked for the Committee's instructions with regard to forthcoming shows, having regard for the fact that such practice entailed the whole time services of three members of the Force and that the horses entered for such shows were not available for ordinary police duty". Not surprisingly it was resolved that in future, no horses be entered for shows of any description without the authority of the Committee. It appeared that the promising show career of the Section had been nipped in the bud. Charles Maby also reported that at an earlier meeting the Chief Constable was authorised to purchase three horses for the mounted police but that these horses had not yet been acquired. It was resolved that the question of the strength of the Mounted Police and the purchase of additional horses be referred to the Finance and Shops Act Sub-Committee for consideration. From this it became apparent that the Mounted Section was under even greater threat than it had been in 1920 and many thought that the 31-year-old unit was facing oblivion. But allies were found in an unexpected quarter.

The following week the Chairman (Alderman Frank Sheppard) stated that the Finance and Shops Act Sub-Committee had considered the question of the numerical strength of the Mounted Police in Bristol, and were of the opinion that no alteration should be made to the authorised strength of 21; and further recommended that as the existing strength was 20 the purchase of an additional horse in respect of which an order had already been given, should be confirmed. It was resolved that the recommendation of the Sub-Committee be adopted. The unit was saved for the moment, but worse was to follow.

In May 1930 severe criticism was levelled at the Branch over police horses being kept for nothing but showing. Alderman Hennessy said he understood that several horses were kept for the International Horse Show, and never went on the street. It was a flagrant waste of money. He was also strongly of the opinion that the strength of the mounted police could be reduced. In reply, Alderman Sheppard said that as to the horses being kept for show purposes, that practice had been stopped. It appears from this that there was some foundation for the criticism, although the training

and preparation for the shows would have resulted in some legitimate withdrawal from ordinary patrol work for the horses involved
with showing. The complaints did nothing to endear the Branch to
councillors opposed to their existence and provided ammunition
with which to exert more pressure for a reduction in strength.
However there was one group in the area for whom the Mounted
Branch was still as popular as ever! The 4th Battalion Gloucester
Regiment again requested use of police horses for a parade in
Ashton Court during May and three horses were subsequently
loaned for the use of the Regiment's officers.

The new Chief Constable's annual report and recommendations
affecting the efficiency and economy of the Force were considered
by the Watch Committee in July 1930. In spite of the earlier support from the Finance Sub-Committee, it was resolved that the
authorised strength of the Mounted Police be reduced to 11; that
the three older horses be destroyed, and five disposed of as and
when possible. Ten officers were to be returned to other duties. The
de-selection process in 1930 was probably a question of ordering a
man to report for beat duty the following Monday, thanking him for
his services to the Mounted Section; but about the same time the
Force invested in 12 BSA motor-cycles in an effort to become more
mobile and Charles Maby arranged for men who had previously
been with the Mounted Section to be assigned to the motor patrols.
And so the unit returned to near foundation levels as the Force
embarked on the decade which saw the rise of Fascism and consequent increase in the potential for street disorder.

Alderman Sir John Swaish, long-time member of the Watch
Committee and its Chairman for 12 years, died on 19th January
1931 and the Mounted Branch had lost another stalwart supporter.

On 23rd February 1932 a meeting of approximately 4,000 people
assembled at the Horsefair to listen to speeches from leaders of the
National Unemployed Workers Union. The crowd was urged to
march to the City Council building, where members of the Council
were discussing plans to reduce unemployment relief rates. As they
moved off in the direction of the Council House the police made no
attempt to hinder the procession but were drawn up in Old Market
Street, with a detachment of Mounted Police in support, ready to disperse the demonstration. When a cordon of police officers prevented

the procession's approach to the Council House they were bombarded with sticks, banner poles, pieces of iron tubing and stones. The
crowd was dispersed by means of baton charges and the use of the
police horses in Old Market, Lawford Street and West Street.

Although Charles Maby later received 15 complaints about
alleged police brutality, the Bristol Trades and Labour Council considered that "the procession was orderly and peaceful, the attack by
the police was entirely unprovoked... mounted police rode on the
pavement down David Street, led by a policeman on a white horse".
Whatever the truth of the matter, the police tactics on the day had
proved extremely successful in breaking up what had become a
riotous gathering: no attempt had been made by the police to prevent
the procession from marching, but they had instead formed ranks on
a site of their own choice to intervene if it became necessary.

In the summer of the same year more demonstrations took place in
Bristol, protesting at the very high rate of unemployment. In early June
a mass meeting was held at Welsh Back which decided to hold a large
procession through the city to Castle Street and Old Market. Permission
to march through these streets had for some time been refused, as it was
the main shopping area. The order was defied by the marchers and
Charles Maby was obliged to send officers out to disperse the procession. The police confronted the march in Castle Street with drawn
batons and some bitter fighting ensued, with the demonstators using
their banners and whatever other weapons they could lay hands on. The
road was like a battlefield when the Mounted Section arrived and can-
tered line abreast along Castle Street, which had the desired effect of
clearing the demonstrators away. Seventy people were treated at the
Bristol Royal Infirmary. No police officers were hurt and no property
was damaged, and no demonstrations were held for a long time after
this event. The following day complaints of police brutality were made,
but these were mostly withdrawn when the Chief Constable allowed the
Press to photograph the offensive weapons left at the scene of the
demonstration. (from *Policing Bristol* by Michael Osborne).

Despite most complaints having been withdrawn, the Council
meeting seized its chance to attack the Branch. Councillor Baston
protested with considerable vigour against the people being "bat-
tered down by the filthy police and the filthy Watch Committee".
There was uproar in the Council Chamber as a result of these

comments. The Watch Committee was required to investigate the complaints and called for a report. Mr Maby dismissed the charges and to add insult to injury as far as the Council Chamber was concerned, his later Annual Report made no reference to the public disorder. However in such volatile times the Council's pragmatism seems to have prevailed, and the use of horses in quelling disturbances seemed to secure the future of the Branch in the short term at least, with opposition voices being temporarily silenced.

In May 1933 the ceremonial aspect of the job came to the fore again, when the Chief Constable reported that members of the Mounted Police had been loaned to the Bath Police Force on the occasion of the visit to Bath of the Duke and Duchess of York (the future King George VI and Queen Elizabeth). He also reported that "an account had been rendered at the usual rates". The Gloucester Regiment was again permitted to borrow four horses both in this year and the following year, and the Committee minutes also note that "repairs to stables and forage store roof at The Shrubbery, Redland, would cost £70". Tenders were invited. Even more prosaic details found their way into the minutes of July 1933, when the Chief Constable reported "that manure from police stables was at present sold to Mr A.J.S.Cousins at a charge of 6d per horse per week, and that Mr Cousins collected the manure when required to do so. He stated that the usual price paid by the Public Assistance Committee was 4s per ton, but that some difficulty was anticipated with regard to the collection of the manure". It appears that the Public Assistance Committee were considering muscling in on Mr Cousins' private individual enterprise, but on this occasion it was resolved to "adhere to the present arrangements"!

In January 1934 police horse *Captain* was certified unfit through being unsound in wind, stiffness and lameness. The animal was taken to the Zoo and destroyed, and a younger horse purchased. Later the same year the Prince of Wales (later the uncrowned King Edward VIII) visited Bristol and, at his own request, no flags were flown and there were no ceremonies. He had come, he said, to see the unemployed. His appearance in various areas of the city drew large and enthusiastic crowds, as befitting the man described as "the best known, and the best loved young man in the English-speaking world". Because of the royal "no ceremony" ruling, the Mounted Branch was relieved of its ceremonial function, but was kept busy all that day in marshalling and restraining the huge crowds. No one then could have foreseen that within two years the Mounted Branch would be required to escort Bristol's Proclamation Coach around the city to celebrate the accession of this popular man's brother.

In 1935 Charles Maby reported that he had received a letter from the Secretary of the Royal Agricultural Society stating that the 1936 Show was to be held at Bristol, and asking whether the Bristol Police would be allowed to support the usual competition class from the Mounted Police. It must have appeared unthinkable

POLICE SUCCESSES AT ROYAL SHOW.—Police Sergeant P. Smith, left, who gained third prize in the class for general turn-out of horse and rider and equipment, at the Royal Show. Police Constable W. King, secured second place in the event for manners and general handiness of the horse as required for its duties.

Press cutting from 1936

that visiting mounted units would compete and escape with trophies in a show held in Bristol without the representation of the local Branch, and this fact, coupled with the Chief Constable's support, persuaded the Committee to relax the veto imposed six years earlier. The unit was once again able to prepare for competition. The Show itself took place on the Royal Showground at Ashton Court between 30th June and 4th July 1936, and was

Mounted Police leading the Bristol Constabulary's Centenary parade, 1936

attended by no less personages than the Duke and Duchess of York and the Lord Mayor of London. Four members of the Mounted Branch competed in the Mounted Police Class, and the following awards were received:
General turn-out of horse, rider, and equipment - 3rd prize: Sgt 5E Percy Smith riding police horse *Clifton*.
Manners and General Handiness of the horse as required for its duties - 2nd prize: PC 56C William King riding police horse *Kilkenny*.

In addition to these successes the event was also significant in breaking the ice for future shows. The following year three horses and men were permitted to compete at the Show again, this time held in Wolverhampton. The Chief Constable was able to report "that 2nd and 3rd places had been awarded to two of the entrants in a class of 34". On this occasion the prizes were won in the turn-out class, with 2nd place awarded to Sgt Percy Smith riding *Goldflake* and 3rd place to PC 116C William Kemp riding *Clifton*. The Committee's congratulations were conveyed to all concerned.

PC Bradley on Bridewell, Central 1937

In 1937 PC Herbert Bradley joined the Mounted Section. Born in 1909, he had performed Army service with the Royal Horse Artillery before joining the Bristol Constabulary in 1936. Twelve months later, after his probationary period, he became a member of the mounted unit at Redland. His expertise and ability with horses was to have a major influence on the Branch, and he soon impressed Sgt Smith sufficiently for him to be entrusted with some of the training of horses and riders. This influence was to increase after the war and became a major factor in Bristol's later show success.

In April 1937 more work was carried out at the Redland stables following a report from the City Valuer to the effect that he had inspected the premises and that repairs to the value of £35 were required "in order to prevent damage to the horses". Some time earlier the roof had been repaired and electric lights installed for the first time. The summer saw the demise of *Victor*, the horse reputed to have been John Watson's favourite. He was certified unfit for further duty in consequence of rheumatism, and he was replaced by a younger animal. The following year two other well-known horses - the bay *James* which had been a prize-winner in 1927, and *Wexford*, were both certified as unfit for further police duty and replaced. *Romulus*, *Jubilee*, and *Bob* were all replaced as the decade came to a close. About this time the strength of the Section was raised by 1 to make a total strength of 12 horses and officers. The unit was to remain at this level for many years to come.

In the years leading up to the end of the decade, part of Percy Smith's duties entailed visiting the various mounted outposts of the city in order to supervise the personnel and horses stationed there. On occasions Percy would take his young son Ronald with him and as Percy was not a driver they used to travel about the city by tram. Many years later Ronald recalled that 5 horses were stabled at Redland (Sgt Smith's home station), 2 at St.George, 2 at Bedminster, 1 at Fishponds, 1 at Horfield and 1 at Sneyd Park. The regular use of the stables at Central was discontinued when the new station was built there about 1930. The use of Fishponds, Horfield and Sneyd Park ceased after the Second World War, when the mounted bases reverted to the three main stations that had been used from the beginning - Redland, Bedminster and St.George.

A Bristol Constabulary General Order dated 5th June 1939 related to the police arrangements for the Annual Combined Church Parade of the RNVR, Territorial Army and Auxiliary Air Force Units, which was to be held later that month on Durdham Downs. It lists the mounted officers who were required to parade at Redland for the event, and those involved were: Sgt 5E Smith; Constables 61A Burgess, 135A Hardacre, 162A Hood, 34B Ashman, 37B Harrison, 36C Linaker, 56C King, and 77C Bradley. It was ordered that "uniform will be as worn on ordinary mounted patrol duty". This was the last peace-time parade supervised by the Branch, and for some of its members - including PC Bradley - it was the last parade before rejoining the colours in preparation for the coming conflict.

As war clouds gathered once more over Europe and the 1930s drew to a close, the Mounted Section of the Bristol Constabulary was able to look back over what had proved to be a tumultuous period for them. It had been a roller-coaster ride of highs and lows, but at least they had the satisfaction of maintaining the unit as a practical arm of the Force. New duties had been accepted, along with confirmation that the work for which they had been originally formed was still relevant in the modern mechanized world.

Would the cautious optimism survive into the '40s, which promised to be at least as unpredictable a decade as the one now passing away?

1940s AND 1950s

On 3rd September 1939 war was declared. Unlike World War I, this war was to place Bristol in the front line, with its reputation for aircraft-building and its busy docks in the city and at Avonmouth. There was a real fear that blanket bombing would soon occur, and arrangements were put in place for the protection of the population. A complete black-out was implemented, air raid procedures were rehearsed, and shelters were dug around the city in an effort to reduce the anticipated casualties from the results of the bombing. In fact the early concern soon diminished as the "Phoney War" rolled on into 1940, and although the war work placed additional responsi- bilities upon the police, life continued much as it had before. Compulsory military service (conscription) was in force, and as the police service was removed as a reserved occupation from November 1939, many officers from the Bristol Constabulary were enlisted in HM Forces, leaving the shortfall in manpower to be made up by the Police War Reserve and the Special Constabulary.

When France fell in 1940, Bristol came well within the range of the German bombers, and on 25th November that year the city suf- fered its first air raid, which lasted for six hours. The centre of the city was the most affected, although damage was also done in the districts of St. Philips, Clifton, Knowle, Bedminster and St.George. The two latter areas housed police horse stables, but fortunately they were spared from the worst ravages of the attack.

Two months earlier, in a demonstration of apparent normality, the local aristocrat Lady Apsley (who resided with her husband Lord Apsley, sometime MP for Bristol NW, at Petty France just outside Bristol) had presented a horse - a mare called *Mary* - to the

Mounted Police in Bristol. The policy of the Branch was then, as it is now, to use only geldings; but on the premise of "not looking a gift horse in the mouth" the animal was accepted. (The horse was never a favourite of Sgt Smith's, who said that she was too small for the job; and in fact *Mary the Mare*", as she became known, only lasted until October 1946 when she was certified unfit for further police service and replaced.)

Baldwin St 1940: Mounted Police lead a War Parade
Note gas mask shoulder straps and Air Raid Shelter sign

The preservation of normality was considered a vital element in the maintenance of morale on the Home Front and initially the continuing use of the Mounted Branch was a thread in the fabric of this policy. The Branch, dressed in patrol uniform but carrying naked swords, would lead the various War Parades through the city. These consisted of Navy, Army and Air Force personnel, marching in all their splendour for National Savings: "Warships Week" or "Wings for Victory Week". However, following further raids by the German Luftwaffe in December 1940 and January 1941, the Chief Constable reviewed the situation and decided that, in the light of increasing enemy hostility, the evacuation of the police horses was desirable.

Consequently, at a Watch Committee meeting on 12th March 1941, the Chief Constable recommended that "owing to the limited use of the Mounted Branch under war conditions and the need for economy in food, the majority of the police horses should be sent to grass from April until the end of September. He had been offered accommodation in a field of about 20 acres that had good keep and water and a large shed for cover, at Cape Farm, Badminton, at a cost of 7s per week for each horse. He stated that if only three horses were employed in turn during the period, the stables at Bedminster and St.George and some at Redland could be closed. Ten men would be released for patrol duty and the estimated cost of horses, harness and forage for the year would be reduced by £100". It was resolved that in the circumstances the Chief Constable's recommendation should be adopted. This was obviously a sensible move in the light of prevailing conditions, with the welfare of the police horses being taken into account in addition to economic considerations. However, once Mr Watts experienced at first hand the work and appetite involved with the maintenance of police horses unexpectedly released into pasture after a period of work in the city, he upped his fees to 10s per horse! This was accepted by the Committee.

Mounted escort for the Prime Minister Winston Churchill, 1941

The evacuation of the horses took place not a minute too soon. March 16th 1941 witnessed what was described as the worst air raid of the war on Bristol, and this was followed by the Good Friday (April 11th) raid which was almost as bad. It was not realized at the time, but in fact this was the last air raid of such intensity to be launched on Bristol. Thereafter single aircraft raids were occasionally endured (and one in August 1942 was particularly horrific as three buses loaded with passengers were set on fire), but the threat to the population was reduced and gradually disappeared as the tide of war turned.

In late 1942 an incident took place which was later referred to by the name "Castle Street Cowboys". The United States had by this time entered the war, and American servicemen, both coloured and white, were stationed in and around Bristol. In an effort to prevent disorder, the authorities designated different "days off" for the coloured and white soldiers, but one night the white soldiers invaded town when it wasn't their turn, and a confrontation became inevitable. A big fight developed between the two groups in Castle Street (by this time largely in ruins except for the Co-op and the Billiard Hall) and when the American Military Police arrived - they joined in! Percy Smith was called down from Redland to Central, where he liaised with Mounted colleagues PCs Harry Hood, Steve Linaker, Fred Hucker and Bill King. Together with their horses they spread across the bottom of Castle Street and charged at the fighting mass. When they reached the top of Castle Street, they turned round and charged down again. By this time the Americans had had enough and disappeared back to their respective quarters. Percy Smith was later heard to comment, "What chance have we got of winning this bloody War, when they run away at the sight of a few horses?"

Although the war went on, life in Bristol returned to comparative normality, and in fact a police horse was actually purchased in August 1943 - *Monty* (named after the famous Field Marshal) for the price of £105. This demonstrated that Chief Constable Maby was already shrewdly deliberating the shape of his post-war Force, and that it was to include a Mounted Section.

It was Sgt. Percy Smith's job not only to seek out replacement horses but to oversee the destruction of horses no longer fit for police duties. These were transported to the Zoo and humanely destroyed in an area near the Upper Belgrave Road entrance. The event was witnessed by Sgt Smith and the Headkeeper in charge of big cats, Tom Fishlock. This policy may seem hard-hearted to us today, but it had been adopted from the beginning as being in the best interests of the animal. No one could afford to keep unfit horses, and their suffering might have increased greatly had they been passed into less skilled or more disreputable hands. Moreover it was acknowledged that horses, being creatures of habit, would not be able to understand why their lifetime of work in a recognised environment was suddenly removed from them, and they would become deeply unhappy and decline as a result.

The current policy, which has been in place for many years now, retires the horses to reputable people with adequate facilities, although the Police Authority always retains ownership. However, it has often been found that the animals do not survive for long once they have finished their working lives. Percy Smith was a good horseman, practical and not given to sentiment. It was not unknown for some choice cuts to find their way from the Zoo to the table in the Smith household, especially during the period of rationing, but whether he actually knew which of his former charges he was now consuming remains debatable!

Peace came in May 1945, and after the victory celebrations the big clear-up operation began, which was to continue for many years. The police horses had all returned to the home stables after their enforced rest, and it must have come as a bit of a shock to again patrol the bustling city after the lengthy period amid the calm environs of Badminton. The Central station had been closed as a regular base for the Mounted Section for many years, but once again the streets around the stations of Redland, Bedminster and St.George echoed with the sound of horses' hooves as they set off on their regular patrols which had been maintained (except for the war intervals) for nearly 50 years.

Police officers who had served in the Forces began to return to reclaim their former employment, and one such was PC 65A Frank Turner, who had served with the Royal Horse Artillery during the War. He had originally joined the Bristol Constabulary in 1938 and was stationed on the Central Division. Like others before him, his interest in horses led him to apply to join the Mounted Section, and in 1946 he was transferred to the unit at Redland. This fulfilled a long-standing ambition that he had demonstrated before the war when he was allowed some leave from his Division to train with the Mounted Branch at Horfield. Now he became a full-time member in the station that traditionally housed the Section's younger horses.

In June 1945 Sgt. Smith led a contingent of mounted officers in heading a procession of members of the Civil Defence Services for a Thanksgiving Service at Bristol Cathedral. The officers concerned were: PCs 34B Ashman; 37B Harrison; 35C Burgess; 56C King; 76C Beck; 14D McDowell; 30D Turner; and 33D Shore. In the days and months following the cessation of hostilities the Section was kept busy escorting similar groups on Thanksgiving parades or supervising the celebrating crowds.

Soon it became possible again to think of horse shows, and in July 1947 one including a class for Mounted Police was arranged at the Memorial Ground, Horfield. Where once there had been opposition to the Branch participating in such events, now there seemed to be whole-hearted support - even for a local Show such as the one in Horfield! Perhaps the very ordinariness and Englishness of it appealed to the authorities, remembering how close they had come, during the dark days of 1940, to losing forever the opportunity to enjoy such an event.

Recalling the Show many years later, Frank Turner related how he had to ride a very young and inexperienced horse in the competition. The animal was so shocked to find itself in the middle of all the activities that it spread its legs and refused to co-operate! It is fair to say that this was one show in which the Bristol Mounted Police did not distinguish themselves; but at least the tradition of competition was reinstated and was to lead in due course to success and a

PC Hardacre on Calidore, Durdham Downs 1947. Note the flat cap

record second to none among the Mounted Sections of the country.

About this time, soon after the end of the War, the Mounted Branch rejected the ordinary police helmet that had been worn for general patrol work, in favour of the flat cap. This was considered to be the smarter item of headwear, and safety considerations did not appear to be a feature in the decision! Apart from the occasions when the ceremonial helmet was used, the flat cap remained standard headwear until 1979, when riding helmets were introduced for the first time.

Between May 1946 and March 1948 four police horses -*Red Rose*, *Duke II*, *Captain*, and *Monty* (the latter being the horse purchased in 1943) were certified unfit for further police duty. As each vacancy occurred, application was made to Mr. Jack James of Quedgeley, Gloucestershire, for replacement animals. Mr. James was an experienced horse dealer, and with his knowledge of what was required in a police horse was usually able to supply the right material. The cost of young bay geldings about this time varied between £110 and £135 each; the animals were always of Irish extraction, and James made frequent visits to Ireland to secure the hunter type which was so sought after in England. He and Percy Smith knew each other well and for many years to come the Bristol police horses were supplied from this source.

In July 1949 the Watch Committee considered the ranks pertaining to the Mounted Branch, and it was resolved that application be made to the Secretary of State for the authorised establishment of the Force to be increased by one Inspector to enable the officer in charge of the Mounted Police to hold that rank. Sgt Percy Smith had passed the examination for promotion, but the establishment of the Branch did not allow for the position of Inspector at the time of this resolution. In fact, the rank of Sergeant had been the senior rank in the department since the time of the First World War. The application from the Watch Committee was either put aside, or not considered at the time, because Percy Smith was not promoted to Inspector until 1955 - six years after the original request. Also in 1949 it was reported that the police horse *Kilkenny*, which had been a prize-winner when ridden by PC Bill King in the famous Bristol Horse Show of 1936, was at the age of 20 years unfit for further police duty and replaced by a younger animal. Similar reports are recorded regarding police horses *Calidore* and *Remus*, and a quote from Mr. Jack James for 2 bay horses at a cost of £125 and £155 respectively was accepted by the Committee.

In November 1950 the Chief Constable reported that a 5-year-old bay gelding *Peter* which had recently been purchased from Jack James had been found to be unsuitable for police work owing to an unnaturalness of action in its hindquarters and limbs. Mr. James redeemed himself by offering to replace the animal with a 4-year-old bay gelding on payment of a further sum of £40. The offer was accepted. In January 1951 the Chief Constable recommended that he should be authorised to enter into an agreement with the proprietors of the Riding School at Eastfield, Westbury-on-Trym, whereby facilities would be provided for the training of mounted policemen, at a cost of £30 per annum. This was in consequence of an instruction that the mounted officers were not to ride on the Downs, where training usually took place, when the conditions were wet. The Eastfield Riding School had the facility of a cinder surface and, although it was an outdoor arena, it could be used in all but the most adverse conditions. For a long time afterwards the regular Tuesday training sessions took place at Eastfield.

Percy Smith leads the unit across the Downs en route to Eastfield for training, for which civilian wear was the custom

In December 1951 Charles Maby reported that the Bristol force had received an invitation to compete at the Metropolitan Police Horse Show to be held in June 1952 and he recommended that the invitation be accepted. This was to be the first Horse Show of national prestige attended by the Bristol Mounted Branch since the War, and it was resolved that the authority be given and for the necessary travelling and subsistence allowance to be paid.

The Show was held at Imber Court, Surrey, on 27th/28th June 1952. Three members of the Branch competed with their horses in the **Best Trained Police Horse Class**, and PC 68D Sam McDowell riding *Shangarry* gained 2nd prize out of 27 competitors. **The Best Trained Class** was designed specifically to show off the qualities required of a police horse and, in addition to a **Best Turnout** competition, consisted of a dressage test (demonstrating the complete control of the rider and obedience of the horse in a variety of movements and paces), and a "street nuisance" test, which subjected the animal to a series of sights, sounds and occurrences which he might meet whilst on patrol, and which he was expected to negotiate without deviating or showing fright. Once again, the Watch Committee conveyed its congratulations to the prizewinning Branch. The tradition of participating in Horse Shows was now firmly established, and was to bring recognition and prestige to the Branch for years to come.

At this time the horses had to be transported about the country by railway as they had been since the very first days of work outside the Bristol area. In the afterglow of the Imber Court success, Charles Maby applied for permission to enquire about the possibility of obtaining some independent means of transportation, and he was duly authorised to make enquiries as to the price of a horsebox. But the acquisition of such a vehicle for the Bristol Constabulary was still some years off. For these first excursions to Imber Court the horses were ridden to Temple Meads Railway Station and placed in an old horsebox carriage for the trip to London. This method meant very long days for the men and the horses, and in fact on one occasion PC Sam McDowell and PC Basil Howells and their horses were shunted into a siding at Reading and were stuck there for eight hours! This unsatisfactory state of affairs continued until it was decided to hire cattle trucks for the purpose of horse transportation, and eventually in 1956 a two-horse trailer was acquired, which was pulled by a van loaned by the Traffic Department.

In 1952 three young officers joined the Branch from their respective Divisions. They were PC Alan Milsom, PC Robbie Collins and PC Frank Knight. They were sent, as was the practice then, to Liverpool (used alternately with Imber Court) to undergo their initial training. The course was of six months' duration, and upon successful conclusion they returned to Bristol to take up their new duties. All three were posted to Redland initially - where Percy Smith could keep an eye on them - and where half the Force's complement of twelve horses was stabled. Four others were kept at St.George, and the two remaining horses were stabled at the impressive police station in East Street, Bedminster. Sgt Smith was still unable to drive motor vehicles, so he maintained his pre-war tradition of visiting the outposts by public transport - except that now it was by bus and not by tram.

His routine for the day was to enter the top stables at Redland at 8.15am (after the officers had mucked-out and groomed) to check the horses, kit and forage barn. Then he would go down to the lower stables at the same station and check the horses and kit kept there. After this he caught a bus to Bridewell, the central police station, went to his office to attend to any reports and paper-work and if necessary liaise with the Superintendent about the work of the Branch. When this was completed, he walked to Old Market and caught a bus to St.George, arriving about 11am in time to check the day-turn mounted officer out on patrol. He then followed the same routine as at Redland, examining horses, kit and stables to ensure a good standard and to sign notebooks and diaries. Then he would see the Chief Inspector at St.George before catching a bus to Bedminster where he would arrive in time

Sgt Smith and PC Bradley on mounted duty in Bristol, 1952

to see the mounted officers come in from their patrol. On the satisfactory completion of his inspection, he boarded a bus for Redland, arriving in time for lunch. The afternoon was often taken up in the tack room at Redland, sometimes in the company of PC Bradley, engaged in the stitching and general maintenance of the saddlery. Percy Smith followed this routine for six days a week unless police operations prevented it, and the men had no excuse for not knowing where he was and what he was doing at any particular time of the day!

Horses came and went, and soon after the Metropolitan Police Horse Show a 5-year-old bay gelding was bought from Jack James for £200. He replaced *Victor*, who was certified as unfit for further police service. Unfortunately the horse - named *Philip* - was only able to register an eight-month career before developing an incurable lameness which resulted in his untimely demise at the Zoo. The same year the Chief Constable submitted a list of riding saddles and bridles to the Watch Committee, which he recommended should be purchased at a cost of £217.16s.0d. and for which provision had been made in the budget. The purchase of the equipment was approved, and the alacrity with which authority was given to spend these sums seemed to demonstrate that the Branch was at last being considered as something more than an optional extra.

In the early '50s one of the local football teams, Bristol Rovers, was drawn against the team of the moment, Newcastle United, in the FA Cup. Following a draw at Newcastle, the First Division team was obliged to return to the Rovers' ground for a replay. On the day tickets went on sale for the match, over 100,000 people crammed into the car park at the Eastville Stadium, and the police horses from St.George were kept busy all that day until late in the evening, marshalling and containing the crowds as they queued for their tickets. The crush was so great that on occasions the mounted officers lifted children up on to the horses to avoid them being overwhelmed.

In 1953 the unit was used to discourage possible unruly behaviour of crowds celebrating the coronation of Queen Elizabeth II in street parties around the city. This was one of the rare occasions that the horses had been used after dark, and stirrup lights were designed for the operation which were powered by batteries stored in the saddle pouches. In later years as more evening football matches were attended, and more night-time police operations involved police horses, the lights were modified and improved in an effort to secure the horses' safety in the dark.

The regular ceremonial mounted escorts, reintroduced after the War, continued to be a feature of the Bristol scene, with perhaps the Rush (Whit) Sunday escort to St.Mary Redcliffe Church being the most spectacular. The officers involved in the 1953 event were: Sgt 5E Smith; PCs 64A White; 37B Weeks; 46C Turner; 74C Pennington; 77C Bradley; 44D Howells; 61D Cotton; and 68D McDowell. The order of dress was: dress tunics; breeches (1948 issue); dress helmets; cross belts; waist belts;

Norman Frost

top boots; brown gloves; and medal ribbons. Cloaks and swords were also carried. In the 1954 escort the same members turned out again, except that PC 81B Pebworth replaced PC Weeks on this occasion. In July of the same year, a contingent from the Bristol Constabulary, including Sgt Percy Smith, PC Herbert Bradley and PC Sam McDowell, went to London to participate in the Royal Review of Police, which took place in Hyde Park in the presence of the Queen. The Order for this event was amongst the last to be signed by the now knighted Sir Charles Maby as Chief Constable and he retired from the Service in September. He had served 45 years in the Bristol Constabulary, 24 of them as its Chief Constable - a remarkable record. Mr. Norman Frost, who had previously been Chief Constable of the Eastbourne Police Force, was appointed as the new Chief Constable and took up his duties immediately.

Amongst the first duties performed by Norman Frost was the approval of the acquisition of a new police horse from Jack James. The horse was to be called *Robin* after Mr. Frost's son. This animal was destined to become one of Bristol's best known police horses because of its later exploits in the showing arena.

In November 1954 Norman Frost reported that police horse *Ranger*, which was 11 years of age and had been attached to the Mounted Branch of the Force for six years and nine months, had

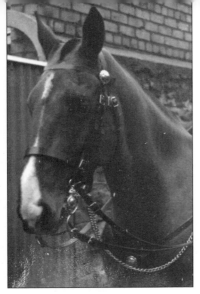
Police horse Ranger in 1954

been observed to be deteriorating, and he had accordingly obtained a quotation from Mr. James for a bay gelding of 5 years of age for the sum of £185 to replace him. He recommended that *Ranger* should be eventually destroyed when the new horse had been fully trained.

However this time the traditional course of events was changed. It was resolved that authority be given for the purchase of the new horse but that the Chief Constable be required to submit a further report on the disposal of *Ranger* with a view to his not being destroyed if a satisfactory home could be found. This represented a major change in policy regarding the disposal of cast police horses, and the thought that the hard-nosed core of the Committee had somehow developed a sentimental attachment to this particular animal does not, somehow, ring true! But it is perhaps indicative of the Committee becoming aware of the as yet unformed idea of the power and importance of "community relations". If there were some soft-hearts among them, however, they must have been gratified to learn from the Chief Constable two weeks later that he had ascertained from the RSPCA that they had a Rest Home for Horses on the Isle of Wight, and that they would be prepared to collect all horses unfit for police work and take them to that Home, free of cost. It was resolved that the Chief Constable be authorised to make arrangements for *Ranger* to be collected by the RSPCA in due course, and sent to the Isle of Wight. Thus was the first horse rescued from "the lion's mouth", and was the beginning of a policy of prolonging the life of retired police horses. It was soon realised that the general public approved of the policy, if only for sentimental reasons.

Not every horse was able to take this route to retirement, nor would it have been right to have thus prolonged the life of animals obviously in distress from some ailment or other. In October 1955 it was discovered that police horse *Danny*, which was 13 years of age and had been attached to the Mounted Branch for nine years and three months, had emphysema of the lungs. As no satisfactory arrangements could be made to retire the horse to a rest home, arrangements were made for the horse to be destroyed. The Watch Committee approved the purchase of a 4-year-old to replace *Danny* at a cost of £190.

The new Chief Constable also decreed that the practice of "hogging" the horses' manes (clipping back to the neck), which had been adopted from an Army tradition, was to cease, and the horses' manes were to be allowed to grow to a natural length and trimmed. This meant that for the following few months the animals sported very proud "centurian crests" as the hair grew back to a length at which it eventually lay flat on their necks!

In 1955 Percy Smith was eventually promoted to Inspector and became the first to hold that rank on the Mounted Branch since the First World War. The vacancy created by Smith's elevation was filled by Herbert Bradley, who was promoted to Sergeant. Bradley was by this time supervising all the training of the horses and officers, and the promotion gave official confirmation to a position he had been occupying for some time. The Rush Sunday escort for that year was performed by: Inspector Smith; Sgt 5E Bradley; PCs 56C Collins; 89C Cockhill; 95C Weeks; 97C Milsom; 44D Howells; 58D Tofts; and 61D Cotton. Two new recruits also joined the Branch that year - PC 112C James Marment and PC 111C Kenneth Bush. They underwent their six month initial equitation course at Liverpool and returned to their posting at Redland, where Jim Marment particularly came under the influence of the newly-promoted Bradley.

It was generally accepted that Sgt Bradley was an outstanding horseman, with abilities and ideas years ahead of his time. This influence, when applied to receptive officers such as Jim Marment and horses such as *Robin*, led to almost immediate success and was soon to reflect in Bristol's pre-eminence on the showing field.

In April 1955, on the recommendation of the Chief Constable, the Watch Committee resolved that police horses should be entered for the Richmond Royal Horse Show to be held between 9th and 11th June. On 15th June Norman Frost reported that three horses had been entered from the Force for the Richmond Show and that Sgt Herbert Bradley, riding police horse *Robin*, had won the Horace Smith Challenge Cup open to the City of London and provincial forces. In addition to the Cup and 1st prize of £10.10s.0d they had qualified for the King George V Champion Challenge Cup which included the Metropolitan police horses, and had been placed 2nd. The following year other successes were reported, when Sgt Bradley on *Robin* was awarded 1st prize, and the Big Ben Challenge Trophy in an Open Competition for the Best Trained Horse at the Metropolitan Police Horse Show, and 4th prize for the Best Trained Horse at the Richmond Horse Show. At the latter event PC Alan Milsom, riding *Artist*, had gained 6th prize. The officers and horses of the Bristol Mounted Branch were beginning to make a name for themselves!

Meanwhile the bread-and-butter work of the Section continued, with patrols of the Downs and other outlying areas of the Divisions maintained, in addition to regular beat work on the city streets. Unless there was a specific operation that demanded it, the horses would not be required to patrol after nightfall because of the risk of accidents occurring due to their presence on the roads. Occasionally however it could not be avoided, and one type of operation that was beginning to require their presence after dark was the attendance at football matches which had an evening kick-off.

For many years mounted officers had attended the two football stadiums in the city, and occasionally rugby's Memorial Ground, fulfilling their role in the supervision of large crowds. The job in those days consisted of marshalling or directing the crowds attending the football games, and as the day of the football hooligan had not yet arrived, the matches at Eastville and Ashton Gate were normally attended by two officers and horses from St.George and Bedminster respectively. Often arrangements were made for the horses to be relieved once the crowd had entered the stadium and the game had begun; such was the peaceful nature of the event. Once in a while four or six horses would be turned out for a match which might attract an especially big crowd - a Cup game, or a local derby between City and Rovers - and on these occasions the local contingent would be reinforced with horses from the Redland stable. In spite of the enormous numbers the events attracted in those days (when it was still a comparatively cheap entertainment) there was little crowd trouble, and in fact Ronald Smith (Percy's son) had no recollection whatsoever that his father had ever attended a football match while on duty or otherwise. The rise of the football hooligan was still a distant ten years off, and spectators were able to enjoy their Saturday afternoon's sport without the unwelcome and dangerous distractions the next generation had to endure.

The year 1956 witnessed the acquisition of the Bristol Constabulary's first horse vehicle. In March the Chief Constable asked for authority to purchase a horse trailer at a total cost of £329. 5s.6d "to enable the speedy transportation of police horses when required". It was resolved by 3 votes to 2 (a narrow majority!) that authority be granted, provided the expenditure could be defrayed out of the existing estimates. The addition of the vehicle to the strength of the Mounted Branch was a great bonus, but many years later Jim Marment recalled that no-one on the Branch was sufficiently talented as a driver to turn the trailer around! He related that when such a manoeuvre was required, the horses would be unloaded from the trailer, which was then unhitched from the towing vehicle and manually turned to face the opposite direction and re-attached, whereupon the horses would be re-loaded and the journey continued. Perhaps the Chief Constable's "speedy transportation of police horses" was a trifle optimistic in such circumstances!

The long career of Inspector Percy Smith was coming to an end and in 1957, in anticipation of the vacancy, Herbert Bradley was promoted to Temporary Inspector and authorised to wear one pip as his badge of rank. (An Inspector normally wears two pips). This created a vacancy on the Branch for the position of Sergeant, and Frank Turner, who had been a member for 11 years, was promoted to fill the gap. In the summer of the same year, the Chief Constable reported that at the Richmond Horse Show, Temporary Inspector Herbert Bradley on police horse *Robin*, had been awarded the **Horace Smith Trophy** and 1st prize of £10.10s.0d. The horse and rider team had then won the **King George V Challenge**

Temporary Inspector Bradley with Robin, 1957

Cup which included the Metropolitan police horses, and he further reported that they had achieved, for the first time ever in such competition, 100% marks - which made *Robin* the perfect police horse.

More heady news of the same type was recorded after the Imber Court Show that year, when Herbert Bradley and *Robin* won the **Big Ben Cup** and 1st prize for the **Best Trained Police Horse**, and PC Alan Milsom riding *Artist* had been placed 5th in the same class and had been highly commended. The Committee recorded their appreciation of the successes.

Towards the end of the year, the Chairman of the Watch Committee, Alderman Knight, reported that he had received a request from the Mangotsfield local council for a detachment from the Bristol Mounted Police to give a demonstration at their Horse Show in June 1958. The Chairman stated that he had given the necessary permission and applied for his action to be confirmed. This was not the first

Inspector Percy Smith

time a request for such a display had been put before the Committee. The previous year approval had been given for the Mounted Section to give a short display on equestrian training at the Searchlight Tattoo held on Durdham Downs in connection with Civil Defence Week, and in the light of this precedent the Chairman's current application was also confirmed. These were the first occasions on which the Branch was used to give riding displays. They later became a regular feature for the unit during the summer months and, in addition to the benefits that came by way of training for officers and horses, were used to enhance the public image of the Force.

During 1958 Inspector Percy Smith retired from the Bristol Constabulary. He had been a member of the Mounted Branch since 1928, and its Horsemaster since 1935. He was described to me as being both a strict disciplinarian and a genuinely nice man, but whatever his qualities he was able to look back on his career with some satisfaction, having confirmed his Commanding Officer's assessment of him when he had left the Royal Horse Guards in 1927 - "should do very well in any post in civil life". He was able to do some judging at Horse Shows during his retirement, which was sadly cut short by his death in 1968. Inspector Bradley was confirmed as the new Horsemaster following Percy's retirement.

L to R: Insp Bradley on Robin; Percy Smith; CC Norman Frost; PC Marment; PC Milsom on Artist, with trophies won in 1959

During the summer of 1958 PC Alan Milsom was absent from work suffering from bouts of pneumonia and pleurisy, so Inspector Bradley instructed his protege PC Jim Marment to take over Alan's horse *Artist* for the period of his absence. During this time *Artist* won the **Best Trained Class** at the Metropolitan Police Horse Show, being awarded the **Big Ben Challenge Trophy**. Jim Marment was later allocated to *Robin*, and competed in the Birmingham Horse Show where they won the **City of Birmingham Perpetual Challenge Bowl** and 1st prize of £5 in the Best Trained class open to police forces outside Birmingham. This qualified them for entry to the Open Championship in which they were placed 3rd. The Committee congratulated PC Marment, and the prize money was paid into the Police Athletic Club.

Tack Room scene at Redland, 1959

In October of the same year the Chief Constable reported that police horse *Shangarry*, one of Bristol's earlier prize-winners, had been found dead following an operation for the removal of an obstruction carried out at the Field Station of the University of Bristol, Langford. The horse had been purchased in 1949 from Jack James at a cost of £155. Authority was given to purchase a replacement.

In 1959 a young Cornishman from Perranporth became a member of the Mounted Section in Bristol, having joined the Constabulary from the RAF two years earlier. His name was Anthony (Nobby) Clarke, and his abilities both in horse training and riding were later to have a big influence in cementing and furthering the Branch's reputation.

1959 also witnessed further success for PC Marment and *Robin* at the Richmond Show. They were placed 2nd in the **Horace Smith Trophy**, qualifying them for entry to the King **George V Challenge Cup**, which they won, coming equal 1st with a City of Bradford police horse. This was the third year in succession that *Robin* had won this trophy, and in October he and Jim Marment took their bow by participating in the Parade of Personalities held at the Horse of the Year Show at the Empire Pool, Wembley. In July the Chief Constable reported that police horse *Artist* ridden by PC Alan Milsom, had been placed 1st in the **Big Ben Challenge Cup** competition at Imber Court, and that this was the second year in succession that *Artist* had been placed first in the Competition.

The Mounted Section's decade closed on a skilful example of crowd management in a situation that could easily have got out of control. It had been the custom for some years to hold a Bonfire Party on the Downs on 5th November, and whereas previous events had passed off peacefully, the police were taken by surprise when the 1958 party had witnessed some trouble. Fireworks had been thrown around, windows were broken and flowers uprooted. On Guy Fawkes Night 1959 preparations were made in an effort to prevent similar problems, and part of the police plan was to utilise the police horses in the area of the party to discourage the unruly element from disrupting the fun. The officers from Redland were on patrol on the Downs from 7pm onwards, but as the evening drew on trouble flared amongst the crowd of 4,000. Fireworks were thrown around, and some were being stubbed out on the horses.

Sgt Frank Turner, who was in charge of the group of six mounted officers (including PCs Frank Knight and Alan Milsom), was struck on the back with a milk bottle as the fighting got worse. The Chief Constable Norman Frost, who was present on the scene, warned the troublemakers that unless they departed from the Downs he would remove them, by force if necessary; but the disorder continued. Norman Frost then gave instructions to Frank Turner for the Mounted contingent to clear the crowd. The unit lined up as a section of six and galloped into the melee. They rode right through the crowd, scattering them, and then wheeled round and rode through again. For several minutes they moved backwards and forwards, breaking up knots of troublemakers until the entire area was clear. The residue was followed down Blackboy Hill into the city to ensure that the trouble did not recur, before the mounted unit was allowed to return to the stables, where they arrived about 1am. Later that night the Chief Constable visited the stables to congratulate the unit on the operation, and a few days later the Chairman of the Watch Committee expressed their appreciation "of the excellent way in which the police had controlled the unruly elements who had congregated on the Downs on 5th November, and it is resolved that the Chief Constable convey the Committee's appreciation of the excellent work done by them on this occasion".

By 1960 the Mounted Section appeared to be in as strong a position as at any time in their history. They were being utilised by a supportive Chief Constable and were rewarding him with a show record which demonstrated that the Constabulary's police horses were amongst the finest in the country. It seemed possible to look forward to the 1960s with a degree of optimism thus far unknown in the history of the unit.

CHAPTER SIX

THE SIXTIES

PC Milsom and Artist training in Ashton Court

In March 1960 the Chief Constable reported that the Planning and Public Works Committee had agreed to the paddocks at Ashton Court estate (recently acquired by the City) being used for the training of police horses, but as yet no rental had been agreed. The following month approval was given for the use of the paddocks at a rent of £75 per annum, with the additional responsibility for maintenance and repairs. This area of Ashton Court then took over from the Eastfield School as the training base for the **Bristol Mounted Police.**

At the same time the Chief Constable reported that he had received an application from the Gloucestershire Constabulary and the British Horse Society for two mounted police to assist at the Badminton Horse Trials for one day only. The application was approved, and so Bristol police horses appeared for the first time at the famous three-day event - but not of course to compete! The cross-country phase of the event was tremendously popular with spectators who swarmed all over the Badminton estate, and it was felt that the supervision of the crowds was best left to police officers on horseback, for whom the job was ideally suited.

In May the police horse *Winston*, which had been acquired in November 1951 for £160, was certified by the Veterinary Surgeon as no longer fit for police duty and was replaced by a 5-year-old chestnut gelding purchased from Jack James for £225. The Chief Constable reported that he was considering whether *Winston* should be loaned indefinitely to Miss Jackie Moore of Dyrham Park Stables, Chippenham who would like the animal as a companion for spastic children. He also intimated that the Horsemaster would visit the stables at Chippenham and ascertain the conditions under which *Winston* would be kept. Approval was given, and *Winston* subsequently spent the remainder of his days at Dyrham Park, to the delight of the disabled children.

In June the Chief Constable reported that police horse *Robin*, ridden by PC James Marment, had been awarded 2nd prize in the **Horace Smith Challenge Cup** and that the pair had subsequently won the **King George V Champion Challenge Cup** for the Best Trained Horse which was open to all police forces, including the Met. This was the fourth successive occasion on which the Cup had been won by *Robin*, and the Watch Committee were invited on a special congratulatory visit to inspect police horses *Robin* and *Artist* and their riders, accompanied by the Horsemaster, Inspector Bradley.

Inspector Bradley on duty with Robin

During September the Chief Constable received a telephone request from the Secretary of the Horse of the Year Show requesting that police horse *Robin* should again lead the Parade of Personalities at the show which was held at the Empire Pool, Wembley in early October. The appearance in the Parade was the only involvement of the police horses in the Horse of the Year Show, because at this time there was no class in the competition for them to enter. This changed in later years and the title **Police Horse of the Year** was to become the most cherished award in the police horse show calendar.

Sgt Frank Turner

Towards the end of 1960 Inspector Bradley retired from the Mounted Section, having completed 25 years service in the police force. There is no doubt that his influence and ability with horses, both in training and riding, inspired the Branch to the pinnacles they had already achieved and were later to attain. The officer certainly had his critics, both in the field of what is now called "man-management" and in connection with the training of the horses, which for some was rather harsh, but he has been described to me as "being the best policeman I ever saw on a horse". The memorial to his career was to be the continuing success of the Branch he worked for. In retirement he and his wife Grace moved to Kent where he continued to work among horses (which remained one of the great loves of his life) and to maintain his high standards in golf which he played off a handicap of three. He died in 1986.

During the interim period after Inspector Bradley's retirement, Sgt Frank Turner was left in charge of the Mounted Branch, but he was assisted by Inspector Jim Lewis before the new appointment was made. Inspector Lewis knew practically nothing about horses and was happy to leave the specialist work to Sgt Turner. However he proved himself an able manager and administrator for the Branch for the nine months of his tenure and the temporary arrangement worked well. In this period he secured riding macs for the unit, which had been long desired, and also started to do a little riding himself!

In June 1961 the Chief Constable reported that "consequent upon the retirement on pension of Inspector Herbert Bradley, an advertisement was published in the Police Press inviting applications for the post of Inspector in Charge of the Mounted and Dog Sections of the Force". (A Dog Section had been formed four years earlier, with the first two handlers, PC Derek Johnston and PC Tom Hornsby, being responsible to the officer head of the Mounted Section). Eight applications were received, and eventually Sgt. Peters from Kingston upon Hull was appointed on 1st July 1961. He was 48 years of age, had 25 years of experience, and for some years had been in charge of the Mounted and Dog Sections of his Force.

At the same meeting Norman Frost reported that police horse *Robin*, ridden by PC Marment, was placed 6th at the Richmond Royal Horse Show. In the same competition police horse *Majesty*, ridden by PC Robinson Collins, had been commended. There had been 23 entries representing 7 police forces. The prize money of £2.2s.0d was paid into the Police Athletic Club. Three days after this event Inspector Bob Peters took up his duties in Bristol and a new era opened for the Mounted Section.

Financial considerations were in the mind of Inspector Peters when soon after his appointment he stopped the practice of sending recruits to Liverpool or Imber Court for their initial equitation courses and instituted such courses "in-Force". This was by far the cheaper alternative and the mounted supervisory became, *ex officio*, the riding instructor. The arrangement suited Sgt Turner, who was a very good horse and rider trainer. From this time all initial courses were conducted within the Branch itself.

In October 1961 the police horse *Timothy* which, like *Robin*, had been named after a son of the Chief Constable, was certified unfit for police duty and subsequently sent to the Zoo. A replacement was authorised. *Robin*, however, was becoming quite a celebrity, with regular invitations to appear at Wembley and requests for "star appearances" at local events in and around the Bristol area. In December the Chief Constable submitted an application for police horse *Robin* to appear at the Berkeley Horse Show in Gloucestershire, which was to be held in August 1962. The Show authorities were prepared to pay a fee of £15.10s.0d for the privilege of having the equine star appear at their event, knowing that the money would probably be recouped at the gate, such was the horse's fame. Permission was granted by the Committee.

The Mounted Section attended even more shows during 1962. The programme for the year was as follows:

Richmond Royal Horse Show - May

Metropolitan Police Horse Show - June

Manchester Flower Show (including a competition for police horses!) - July

City of Birmingham Horse Show - August

The Hull Horse Show - August.

This amounted to two more shows than the previous year, and perhaps demonstrated that the Watch Committee was developing a taste for the showing success of the Section. The show at Hull was doubtless submitted for approval because of the influence of the newly-promoted Inspector Peters who would have been anxious to show off his new charges to his former colleagues in that city! It was important that the Bristol horses kept up their winning ways this particular year, because a new competition was to be instituted as part of October's Horse of the Year Show, entitled "**Police Horse of the Year**". This competition was open to police horses which had managed to achieve 1st, 2nd or 3rd place in a Police Horse Show held during 1962.

As things turned out, Bristol had to wait until the Birmingham Show before the objective of qualification was achieved, but it was well worth waiting for. In September the Chief Constable reported that "at the Birmingham Horse Show on 31st August an outstanding success was achieved by police horse *Robin* ridden by PC 112C Marment. In the competition for **Best Trained Police Horse** open to all forces in the country (except Birmingham) *Robin* was awarded 1st place with 100% marks". 19 horses from ten forces had competed. As a result, *Robin* was entered in a competition for the **Best Trained Police Horse** confined to the first three successful competitors in the previous competition, together with horses from the City of Birmingham Police Force. *Robin* won this and was declared **Midland Champion**. This success entitled the horse to entry in the new Police Horse of the Year competition. The success which the Bristol police horses had attained thus far is even more remarkable when compared to the size of the units available to their main competitors: Birmingham had a stable of over 50 horses, and the Metropolitan Police, with whom the Bristol contingent had also been in competition, were able to select from over 200 horses.

During the summer of 1962 another equine recruit was brought to the Redland stables which was destined to step into *Robin's* hoof-prints and bring further success for the Bristol outfit. He was named *Redcliffe* after the beautiful church and area in the centre of the city, and his initial training was entrusted to Sgt Turner and PC Tony Clarke.

The inaugural Police Horse Class of the Horse of the Year Show was to prove something of an anticlimax for the Bristol unit and the Force. *Robin* ridden by Jim Marment was placed 3rd in the competition, after being one of the favourites for the title at the beginning of the event. After doing well in the dressage phase of the competition, the horse was less steady in the unfamiliar atmosphere created in the indoor arena where the nuisance phase was held, and he jumped at the prostrate dummy on the ground, perhaps startled by the bright lights reflecting on the dummy's silver buttons. This first competition was won by a horse from the City of Birmingham Police Force. Winning this class was going to be harder for the Bristol entries than had been anticipated! It was not to be long though before the name of a Bristol horse graced the trophy which, in time, they came to dominate.

This setback did not lessen *Robin's* appeal as a crowd puller. In February 1963 the Chief Constable reported that he had received an application from the North Somerset Agricultural Society for the horse to give an equitation display at their annual show at Ashton Court, to be held on 3rd June 1963. The cost of the demonstration would be £15.1s.6d, which the Society had agreed to pay. He therefore recommended that agreement be given for the demonstration to go ahead and the Committee resolved accordingly. At the same meeting it was agreed that the police horses would attend the following shows:
Stafford Horse Show - May
Richmond Royal Horse Show - June
Metropolitan Police Horse Show - June
Manchester Horse Show - July
City of Birmingham Horse Show - August.
These shows, together with the Horse of the Year Show at Wembley, were to be the main events patronised by the Bristol Branch during the ensuing years.

In March 1963 an echo of the past returned, when the Duke of Beaufort, Colonel of the Royal Gloucestershire Hussars, requested the loan of 5 police horses in April in connection with the presentation of the Freedom of the City of Gloucester to that Regiment. The Watch Committee agreed to the loan of the 5 horses at a cost of £15.15s.0d.

In May another long-time member of the Branch, police horse *Paddy*, which had been purchased in 1946 for £110, was, at the age of 22 years, certified unfit for further police duty. It was recommended, and subsequently approved, that *Paddy* should be sent to Dyrham Park as a companion for former police horse *Winston*, as the facilities at the establishment there were excellent. A 4-year-old bay gelding was bought from Jack James for £300 as a replacement for *Paddy*.

Ordinary patrol work continued for the Section, and regular attention to the Downs area remained the responsibility of the horses at Redland. The first mounted unit out from the early turn group always covered the Downs, with the officer using his horse to patrol between the bushes and into some of the more inaccessible parts of the locality. During the summer a second mounted patrol would be detailed to cover the perimeter of Bristol Zoo, which was a major attraction for thousands of people from around the region and further afield. The mounted officer would assist in the vicinity of the car parks and coach parks to help ease the congestion and discourage car-theft and vandalism. The units at St.George and Bedminster patrolled the built-up areas and shopping centres on their own Divisions, maintaining the high profile policing to which the population in their locality had become accustomed.

In addition to the regular turn-out for football matches and ceremonial duties, mounted units were also required to police the annual Bristol University Rag Procession through the city. At this time the Rag Procession (the culmination of Rag Week during which students raised money for charitable purposes) was a big attraction, and hundreds would throng the pavements to watch it go by. The traditional high jinks of the event were always much in evidence and the mounted officers had to keep a wary eye open for some trick to be played on them as they assisted the students' progression through the streets. It would be difficult to surmise what the horses thought about the whole business as bags of flour hurtled past their noses, but at least the experience was a good preparation for the part they were later required to play in escorting the Somerset Winter Carnivals!

During one Rag Procession Sgt Frank Turner was on *Redcliffe* in the vicinity of the Victoria Rooms in Clifton, when he saw some students trying to pour soap powder into the ornamental fountain. Frank Turner tried to move *Redcliffe* forward to prevent the irritating jape, but to his surprise the horse, who had already achieved a reputation for boldness, refused to move one step. He tried to urge *Redcliffe* forward again, this time more forcefully, and once again *Redcliffe* refused to move. Puzzled, Frank Turner looked down at the horse's front legs; and there, hugging *Redcliffe's* knees in a blissful embrace, was a small child. Frank may have been unaware of the child's presence, but the horse had realized that to obey his rider's instructions on this occasion would result in injury to his little admirer and had therefore remained stock-still...

In August 1963 the Chief Constable was able to report further success for *Robin* and Jim Marment. At the Richmond Royal Horse Show the pair had come equal 1st in the **Best Trained Police Horse** class and had thereby qualified for entry to the Horse of the Year Show to be held at Wembley on 1st October. It was resolved that *Robin* be entered for the Show forthwith. Another police horse, *Clifton*, was reported as being "no longer fit for police work due to lameness in both feet." (sic!) It was resolved that the animal be destroyed and replaced.

The Horse of the Year Show was to prove a fruitless venture for *Robin* once again, and in fact throughout his illustrious career he never achieved the accolade which the last show of the season bestowed. However in his case it hardly seemed necessary to add this distinction to a list of successes which was by now impressively long. Even today, this horse remains one of Bristol's best remembered animals. The title was soon to belong to Bristol, but it was the younger horse *Redcliffe* who eventually carried off the prize, thus helping to maintain Bristol's winning reputation.

George Twist

On 16th March 1964 the Chief Constable Norman Frost retired from the service, having completed almost ten years in the post. Mr. George Twist, the former Assistant Chief Constable of the Liverpool Police Force, who attended his first Watch Committee meeting on 25th March that year, succeeded him. He was destined to become the last Chief Constable of the Bristol Constabulary.

In July George Twist reported that police horse *Beaufort*, an 8-year-old gelding purchased in September 1960 for £185, had developed a vice of rearing when performing duty in traffic, and had therefore become a danger. In addition the horse had recurring lameness in both front legs and was no longer suitable for police purposes. The Chief Constable stated that he had now obtained a 4-year-old chestnut gelding on trial, which had been reported as suitable and sound by the Veterinary Surgeon. The cost was £300, but Mr. James of Quedgeley, who owned the horse, was prepared to accept *Beaufort* in part-exchange, allowing the Committee £50. It was resolved that the exchange be accepted.

During November the police horse *Majesty*, which had been a prize-winner when ridden by PC Robbie Collins at the 1961 Richmond Show, developed an unsound heart and respiratory disorder which necessitated having the animal destroyed. Another chestnut gelding was acquired from Jack James for the sum of £300 which, after a satisfactory trial and examination by the Veterinary Surgeon, replaced *Majesty* on the Branch.

Police horse Majesty at Redland

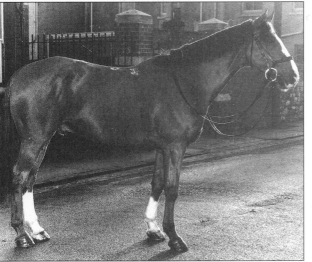

In June 1965 a new name appeared on the list of champion Bristol police horses. The Chief Constable reported that "police horse *Redcliffe*, ridden by PC 106C Tony Clarke, had been placed first in the **Horace Smith Challenge Cup** for the Best Trained Police Horse at the Richmond

Royal Horse Show on 10th June 1965. This event is open to all police horses in the British Isles (excluding the Metropolitan Police, for whom another class is held). The winners and runners-up from these two competitions qualify to enter for the **King George V Champion Challenge Cup** and police horse *Redcliffe* was placed 1st and won the latter Cup." Inspector Peters and PC Tony Clarke attended the meeting and the Chairman congratulated them upon this outstanding achievement. The Chief Constable reported that *Redcliffe* would take part in the Annual Inspection of the Force to be held on the following day and the Committee requested that the Chief Constable make arrangements for the two Cups to be on display at the function.

The following month *Redcliffe* demonstrated that his victory was no flash in the pan by further success at Manchester, where he came 1st in the Manchester Police Horse Show. This now made him eligible for entry into the Horse of the Year Show. *Redcliffe* was developing well, and in fact was placed 2nd in the 1965 **Police Horse of the Year**, but the best was yet to come from *Robin's* worthy successor. And even as *Redcliffe* was beginning to make a name for himself, the Bristol stable acquired another animal which was later to become another major show champion - a liver chestnut gelding called *Avon*.

In January 1966 the Chief Constable reported that police horse *Artist*, which was now 18 years of age and had been a regular prizewinner a few years earlier, had retired to the RSPCA Home on the Isle of Wight, and recommended that the animal be replaced by a bay gelding from Jack James which would cost £330. The Watch Committee approved the purchase and further resolved that Bristol police horses should attend the same six horse shows as in the previous year. The expectation was, by this time, that the season would bring a substantial success to the Bristol Force in the competitive world. The expectation was not disappointed. *Redcliffe* qualified for the Wembley show several times during the year when he achieved 2nd place at Stafford, 3rd place at Richmond, 3rd place at Liverpool and 3rd at the Metropolitan Police Horse Show at Imber Court. During all these successes the horse was ridden by PC Tony Clarke and the pair were obviously saving the best for last. The 1966 Horse of the Year Show finally, and inevitably, accorded a Bristol horse the accolade **Police Horse of the Year**, when *Redcliffe* and PC Clarke were awarded 1st prize. The spotlight which was falling on the successful competition teams also reflected well on the work being carried on day-to-day on the streets, as the Bristol public became more aware of the excellence of the horses patrolling in their midst.

Earlier in the year attention had been given to the possibility of re-housing the Mounted and Dog Sections in one establishment, as this was considered to be a more efficient way of supervising and operating the units. It had been accepted for some time that the small yard at Redland was totally inadequate for the uses to which it was being put, including the training of the young

PC Clarke on Redcliffe with Inspector Peters and Horse of the Year Show trophy 1966

horses, and the yards at St.George and Bedminster were no better situated. Various sites were being considered, including one at Hotwell Road and another in Ashton Court. At a meeting in September 1966, the Chairman of the Committee referred to the difficulties experienced in obtaining a site at Hotwell Road, and he outlined "the need for a centralised Mounted and Dog training headquarters, which could be established at Ashton Court. Ample paddock space is available for training horses and dogs, and considerable advantages would be gained by centralisation instead of operating three separate establishments."

Stable yard at Redland

The City Architect informed the Committee that the proposed scheme, which would provide facilities for training twelve horses and six dogs, was estimated to cost £52,000, including professional and supervisory fees. It was resolved that the Hotwell scheme be deleted from the building programme and the establishment of a mounted and dog training headquarters at Ashton Court be approved in principle, subject to the approval of the Home Office. The possibility of Ashton Court becoming the new base for the police horses increased when in October the Chief Constable reported "regarding the proposed Mounted and Dog Section building at Ashton Court, he had been informed by the City Engineer that the Planning and Public Works Committee had agreed that the lease to the Watch Committee of the paddocks and adjacent buildings at Ashton Court estate be extended for a period of 21 years to 99 years, subject to the buildings and layout being carried out in a manner appropriate to the setting." It seemed that it would be only a matter of time before the police horses could call the lovely estate at Ashton Court their home, but subsequent examination of the site revealed some major problems.

In January 1967 the Chief Constable, City Architect and members of the Watch Committee inspected the site. The existing buildings were in an advanced state of disrepair. The City Architect outlined the plans of the new scheme, which involved major demolition, and he described the approximate area of the site, which would accommodate the new buildings. The whole site was so run down that the Committee became less than enthusiastic about its use for the two units. Further complications arose in the shape of local residents' objections and a Home Office requirement that the site be "appropriated" instead of leased (a requirement with which the Planning and Public Works Committee were not prepared to comply). As a result the Committee began to look around at other possibilities, including sites at Kingsweston, and at Clifton Bridge Railway Station, Bower Ashton.

The end of the Committee's interest in the Ashton Court site also terminated a proposal made earlier in the year that when the new Mounted and Dog Section headquarters was provided, the unit could undertake responsibility for the maintenance of the Lord Mayor's Coach and horses. It was considered that an economy could thereby be made in the budget of the Lord Mayor and Sheriff's Committee without imposing additional financial burdens on the Watch Committee. The proposal actually went as far as the Home Office, who replied that "there was no objection to the Horse master undertaking these additional responsibilities on the understanding that the duties would occupy only a small proportion of police time. The position should be kept under review". It was perhaps just as well that the whole idea sank without trace following the demise of the Ashton Court project.

In December 1966 it was proposed that the officer in charge of the Mounted and Dog Sections should be upgraded from Inspector to Chief Inspector. The officer's responsibilities had increased considerably in recent years and would become even more onerous in April 1967 when the Dog Section establishment was to be increased by the addition of 5 handlers and dogs. The officer would then have under his command in the Mounted Section one sergeant, 15 Constables and 12 horses; and in the Dog Section, one sergeant, 20 Constables and 21 dogs.

It was recommended that this proposal be implemented with effect from 1st April 1967, subject to the approval of the Secretary of State. This promotion for Inspector Peters was later deferred until July 1967, "after the expiration of the period of severe restraint". However from July the promotion was confirmed and for the first time a Chief Inspector headed the Mounted Section.

In May 1967 permission was granted for *Redcliffe* and *Robin* to take part in a cavalcade of horses at the forthcoming Royal Cornwall Show, at a cost of £75, to be met by the Royal Cornwall Agricultural Association. Then in June the Royal Gloucestershire Hussars applied for the loan of two police horses to be ridden by their officers in the Cheltenham Tattoo. The horses would be required for one hour each evening and afternoon performance and accommodation would be provided with horses of the Household Cavalry at Leckhampton. The loan was approved subject to the payment of expenses estimated at £16.16s.0d, and the police authority being indemnified against third party risks and death or injury to the horses. This was one of the last occasions that police horses were lent out to the soldiers at Gloucester, and a change in policy regarding the use of police horses finally ended the link between the two establishments which had gone back to 1922.

The following month there was an application from the Honorary Secretary of the Wedmore Harvest Home requesting a display by the police horses on the occasion of their Harvest Home in August. In reply to the Committee's questions the Chief

Bristol police horses performing at Wedmore Harvest Home, 1967

Constable confirmed that a limit was fixed each year for the number of displays to be given by the Mounted Section, and it was subsequently agreed that four horses should give a display for a charge
of £28. Although events such as the ones in Cornwall, Cheltenham
and Wedmore brought revenue into the Force, the employment of
the horses for such non-police purposes was beginning to cause
concern to some members of the Watch Committee, who ques-
tioned the maintenance of the unit for such events during a period
of tight monetary constraints.

In November 1967 discussions about possible sites for the new
Mounted and Dog Section headquarters began again. This time
Clifton Bridge Railway Station was considered, but there was a draw-
back in that the railway authorities wanted to retain a portion of the
land, as well as access to that portion. The Chief Constable (with
Chief Inspector Peters' support) stated that he considered a far more
suitable site would be at Kingsweston, on land near the police station
at Napier Miles Road. However, subsequent Planning Committee
objections concerning the land there being zoned as "public open
space" redirected the interest back to Bower Ashton, and the
Committee subsequently purchased the Clifton Bridge Railway
Station site. In response to a Home Office query, the Committee's
secretary recorded that they had "purchased Clifton Bridge Station
from British Railways for planning purposes to ensure that any development carried out on the site of the Station is of a low density which
would not be at variance with the Council's desire to retain the open
views of the Suspension Bridge and the Avon Gorge". They also
agreed to the appropriation of the land for police purposes (which

they had been unwilling to do on the Ashton Court estate) and stated that the proposed buildings would meet their requirements on planning grounds. Thus plans went ahead for the headquarters and exercise paddock to be situated at Bower Ashton.

PC Marment on Redcliffe, Horse of the Year Show 1967

During 1967 a reallocation of horses saw PC Jim Marment teamed up with *Redcliffe*, and PC Tony Clarke with *Avon*. They became the Bristol Constabulary representatives at the 1967 Horse of the Year Show. The police horse class was to prove a triumph for Bristol as *Redcliffe* was placed 1st for the second year running, and *Avon* proved his potential by coming a worthy 2nd. Then in the Inter-Constabulary Pairs Competition (in which the two horses performed the dressage and nuisance tests together as a team) they were again placed 1st. Further success followed at the Birmingham Horse Show in 1968 when *Avon*, ridden by PC 43C John Burgess, was awarded 1st place and the **Birmingham Challenge Bowl**. The same pair were later placed 3rd in the **Midland Championship,** in which 27 entries from 10 police forces had taken part.

GREETINGS TELEGRAM ❋

2084 AP8 11.50 BRISTOL J ALLPURPOSE

HORSEMASTER REDLAND POLICE BRISTOL-6 ▪

CONGRATULATIONS REDCLIFFE AND AVON FIRST AND SECOND

POLICE HORSES OF THE YEAR ▪

PROUD BRISTOLIANS ✦

Greetings telegram from 'Proud Bristolians'

In early 1969 the increasing use made of the police horses at events outside the Bristol area once again brought up the question of transportation. The two-horse trailer purchased in 1956 had performed sterling service and would do so for several more years yet, but occasionally the need to move more than two horses at one time high-lighted the Section's inefficient transport arrangements. Consequently in April the Chief Constable reported that an order had been placed for a Bedford 4-stall horsebox at a cost of £3161. After its arrival the unit was enabled to transport half of its strength at once, and this was soon to be of great value.

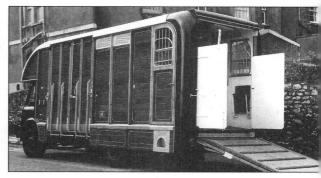

The new Bedford horsebox 1969

During the summer of 1969 *Robin* was, at the age of 19 years, retired from the service. He went to the RSPCA Home on the Isle of Wight, but enjoyed less than a year's freedom before an altercation with a pony left him with a damaged shoulder. There was no alternative but to put the horse down. In spite of his show successes, *Robin* was not the easiest horse to handle and many a groom feared for his life when entering a stall with him! However, his demise was mourned back at his old stable in Redland and his position was considered secure in the annals of Bristol's Mounted Section.

That the Bristol public were aware of the show-winning potential of their police horses there is no doubt; the results of the shows were always well reported in the local press, and occasionally whole pages were devoted to the unit which featured facets of its day-to-day life. But the straitened circumstances in which the nation found itself in the late '60s also gave rise to criticism of the way public money was being spent. Occasionally the old argument about the relevance of police horses, still seen by some as an anachronism, was being raised in certain quarters. Critics of the unit pointed to the fact that only a limited amount of police work could be done from the back of a horse. It was argued that while the value of police horses in public disorder situations was undisputed, incidents of such disorder were (unlike London where the mounted contingent had just had to endure the anti-American Grosvenor Square riots) rare in the West Country, and did not justify the maintenance of a full-time Mounted Branch. Sometimes it seemed that the horses' high-profile success at the Horse Shows merely illuminated them as a target for their more vociferous opponents.

Some criticism was also being heard in the debating chambers of the City Council, especially when the question of the allocation of money for the unit for new headquarters or replacement animals was being discussed. The Mounted Section was once again having to provide arguments for their retention as a permanent Branch of the Force; but as the Sixties drew to a close, new and often intimidating challenges to the Bristol Constabulary arose in the shape of football hooliganism, which was to give the Force ample justification in maintaining its Mounted Branch.

Of more immediate concern was the arrival on tour of the Springboks rugby team from the apartheid-blighted nation of South Africa. Advantage was quickly taken of the four-horsebox facility when urgent requests were received from the Gwent Constabulary and Devon and Cornwall Constabulary for the Mounted Section to assist in the policing of the controversial tour.

Public attitudes to authority, especially among the post-war generation, were changing fast. Global communications had brought the problems and injustices of governments around the world into prominence as never before, and the police suddenly found themselves having to cope with massed street protests. Together with Vietnam and "Ban-the-Bomb", the anti-apartheid issue was a particularly emotive one, and thus the rugby team unfortunate enough to carry the name of South Africa was an obvious target for demonstrations. In November 1969, at the request of the Chief Constable of the Gwent Constabulary, members of the Mounted Branch including Chief Inspector Peters, Sgt Ken Bush (who had replaced Frank Turner upon the latter's retirement earlier in the year) and six constables went to Newport to be available in case of serious disturbances resulting from the rugby match between Newport and the Springboks.

The officers and horses were used all day in support of police officers who were manning barriers, with the intention of preventing any of the demonstrators from approaching too close to the rugby ground. The roads around the ground were quite narrow, which assisted in the operation; and Alan Milsom, recalling the situation, remembers that the first indication that the protesters were on their way was a noise like a train in the far distance which gradually became louder and louder until the chanting crowd appeared around a corner in front of them. The police operation that day succeeded in preventing the protesters from stopping the game, which went ahead as planned; and a week later mounted units were in action again at Ebbw Vale for a second Springboks match in the Valleys. Here one of the main routes to the ground was over a road bridge, which was just wide enough to take four of the police horses abreast, and once again this formidable barrier deterred the demonstrators from achieving their aim. The horses were used again to assist in maintaining order at a Springboks match at Exeter just after Christmas, when a small demonstration was peacefully contained.

On the last day of the year the Mounted Section turned out in force to patrol the area around the Memorial Ground in Horfield, where a Western Counties XV were entertaining the visitors. As the demonstrators could approach the ground from any one of a number of directions, the match was considered especially vulnerable. Mutual aid from the surrounding forces was invoked, and mounted officers were deployed in pairs to cover the area. This was at a time just before personal radios became available to the Mounted Section and the officers would have been obliged to deal with whatever occurred in front of them without being able to call for back-up. As it transpired, the demonstration was a peaceful one, with the only disruption occurring when a man ran on to the pitch at half-time to spread a quantity of carpet nails on the playing area.

The 1960s ended with a fore-taste of operations that were to become the norm as violence flared at football grounds around the country. The hooligans of society leapt upon the anonymity and potential animosity in football crowds to provide cover for their warped entertainment, and while the game of football suffered, the police horses suddenly came into their own as police commanders sought to maintain order in and around the grounds. The emphasis was "crowd control", and in this the mounted unit had an invaluable role to play.

Mounted officers on duty at Newport for Springboks match. Sgt Bush front left. Note the 'riot chains'attached to horses' bits to act as uncuttable reins

CHAPTER SEVEN

1970 - 1980

In January 1970 Chief Inspector Bob Peters retired, having completed nearly 35 years police service. The following month the Chief Constable reported to the Watch Committee that following the retirement of Chief Inspector Peters the post of Horsemaster had been advertised, and from a short list prepared he had selected Inspector Richard Cheetham of the Birmingham City Police. Richard Cheetham was attending a course at the Police College, and could take up the appointment upon promotion to Chief Inspector on 1st April 1970. This was the same day that Sgt Brian Langley of the Dog Section was due to be promoted to Inspector and take up his duties as second in command to the mounted Chief Inspector. The Mounted and Dog Sections hierarchy was thus established in the form it was to retain for the next 23 years.

In March work began on building the Mounted and Dog Sections headquarters at Bower Ashton. This involved the demolition of the existing railway station buildings, and the levelling and treatment of the site. The accommodation to be provided included administrative offices and staff rooms, a kennel block, stable and storage block, harness rooms, bulk storage facilities and a garage. The buildings were to be arranged to form an enclosed courtyard and occupy an area of 1.18 acres and the remaining area of 1.8 acres was to be used as an exercise paddock. Soon afterwards work began on the surveying and preparation of the site at Bower Ashton.

The extent to which the police horses had been used during the recent Springboks tour demonstrated once again their effectiveness in that type of situation and, with disorder becoming increasingly common at football matches, the mounted units were being increasingly called upon. However it soon became apparent that additional training and planning for the use of the horses in crowd situations was becoming necessary.

Up until this time, the only formal crowd control training consisted of the horse being ridden past a few officers who would be waving banners or banging drums, and a manoeuvre known as "closing up on the coach". This consisted of the mounted officers who were performing escort at the rear of the mayoral coach, riding up alongside the vehicle in order to protect the occupants from any attack. What was now required was a controlled training situation which involved a real "crowd", that is several dozen people, so that the horses could be trained to accept a variety of manoeuvres and dispositions while facing a "real" and noisy opposition. Chief Inspector Cheetham was given the task of finding a local establishment that would be willing and able to provide such a body of people to make up a crowd, and the Army Apprentices College, whose buildings lay just across the Severn Bridge at Chepstow, provided the answer. So started a public order training programme with the assistance of the army apprentices, and new approaches began to be worked out for the safest and most effective employment of horses in the crowd situation.

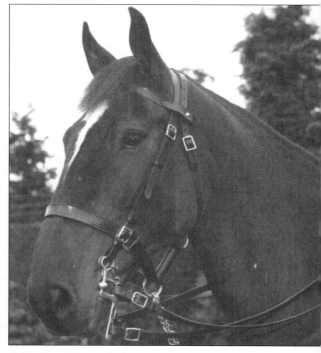

In July 1970 police horse *Blaise*, which had been purchased in 1963, was diagnosed as suffering from acute respiratory trouble, and the Veterinary Surgeon recommended that the animal be destroyed. A replacement was purchased from Jack James for £400. The magnificent Georgian building Kingsweston House had

Police horse Kingsweston

recently been acquired by the City Council, and members of the Watch Committee suggested that the new horse might be called *Kingsweston*. This was approved and adopted, and the name was soon to be heard around the showgrounds of the country as the horse developed into another of Bristol's champion animals.

Two horses were entered for the Police Horse of the Year class at Wembley in October when *Avon*, ridden by PC Joe Grace, achieved 2nd place. In the Pairs competition they were joined by *St.Michael*, ridden by PC Jim Marment, and this time they went one better by being awarded 1st place and declared Inter-Constabulary Pairs Champions.

Preparations commenced with the New Year to transfer all the horses and mounted equipment from Redland, St. George and Bedminster to the headquarters being built at Bower Ashton. Interest in the new site was naturally high amongst the mounted officers, but they were also saddened to be moving from their traditional bases which had served them and their predecessors well since the turn of the century. It was certainly true that the unit needed a new home, especially one which was able to offer an adjacent exercise and training area, in addition to the proximity of the Ashton Court estate; but some felt that the centralisation on the outskirts of the city would inevitably mean less cover for some areas which would be too far distant from the new base for ordinary mounted patrols. This was answered in part by planning for "box patrols" - loading the horses and officers into the horsebox, together with all their equipment, transporting them to a point some miles distant, and dropping them off to patrol the area before heading back towards Bower Ashton. In spite of these plans, many residents in the vicinity of the old stables regretted the move away from their neighbourhood, as much for the removal of old friends as for the inevitable reduction in uniform patrols that the move would bring.

In April 1971 the Chief Constable obtained grazing land for his horses which had formerly been the Osier and Kitchen Garden Fields at Ashton Court. The rent until the end of the year was £80, and was a far more convenient arrangement than the use of the paddock in Ashton Court, which had been arranged in 1960.

In June there were more show successes to report. At the South of England Horse Show (the former Richmond Royal Horse Show) held at Ardingly, Sussex, the Bristol Constabulary had entered police horses *Avon*, ridden by PC Joe Grace, and *St.Michael*, ridden by PC Jim Marment. In the Show *Avon* won both the **Horace Smith Challenge Cup** (open to provincial forces) and the **King George V Cup** for the Best Trained Police Horse (open to all police forces). *St.Michael* had been placed 3rd in the Horace Smith Challenge Cup Competition.

As the showing season progressed Bristol's success showed no sign of diminishing! In Manchester the following month, *Mayfield* ridden by PC 28B Raymond Gilbert was placed 1st in the Trainer and Handy Horse Competition in which there was an entry of 30 competitors from 15 police forces. In the class for the Best Trained Horse, *St.Michael* was placed 5th out of 42 horses. Later the same month, at the Metropolitan Police Horse Show, *Avon* (PC Joe Grace) won the **Big Ben Challenge Cup** by coming 1st in the provincial competition and then won the **Championship Challenge Cup** against the winners of the Metropolitan class. Then in Birmingham, *Avon* (PC Joe Grace) and *St.Michael* (PC Jim Marment) were placed 2nd and 3rd respectively in the Best Trained class open to forces outside Birmingham. In the Midland Championship, competed for by the first four in the provincial class

Training for a Musical Ride

and the first two in the Birmingham class, *St.Michael* gained 1st place and *Avon* 2nd. It was apparent that the Bristol horses and riders were the current leaders amongst the country's mounted police, and the force took great pride in the achievements of the unit.

Police horse negotiating a 'nuisance' at a community event

In addition to the showing circuit, the summer brought with it requests for the Mounted Branch to give riding displays to various groups around the region. The number of displays were deliberately limited so that the time taken in rehearsal and execution would not impinge on officers' patrol time or interfere with any police operations which would always have priority, but the advantage gained in terms of public goodwill was considered to be worth the time taken.

In June 1971, for example, the branch was invited to stage a display at the Dairy Festival in Weston super Mare - at a cost to the festival of £100. The invitation was approved, and a "Musical Ride" was prepared for the event. This consisted of four horses and riders performing dressage movements to the accompaniment of music of an appropriate beat. Similar Rides had been given for some years for the more major events, although sometimes one or two horses would perform displays which included a "nuisance lane" as an exhibition for events of more modest proportions. The time taken in preparation for such activities was justified as being part of the necessary training for riders and horses, as well as fulfilling a vital community relations role. In fact, the attraction of the riding displays further spread the reputation of the mounted unit. Later that year the unit was also given

Mounted and Dog Sections new headquarters at Bower Ashton, 1971

permission to perform displays at the Southsea Show during August, and at the Dorchester Agricultural Show in September. The costs in respect of travelling expenses, pay and allowances were charged to the promoters concerned, who appeared happy to pay not inconsiderable sums for the privilege of having the famous Bristol police horses performing at their functions.

The Mounted and Dog Sections' new headquarters at Clanage Road, Bower Ashton, finally came into operational use during August, and the stables around the city closed their

PC Milsom on Prince with the Duke of Beaufort and Chief Inspector Cheetham

doors to the horses for the last time - although Redland later played host to two police horses for a while when space was required at Bower Ashton. The buildings themselves were of box-like construction, with flat roofs (which later leaked incessantly) and drains which soon proved inadequate and caused problems for many months to come. From an aesthetic point of view the establishment looked good, in keeping with the Council's laudable desire to maintain the pleasant aspect of the Suspension Bridge and the Avon Gorge. There were, however, features of its construction which were not appreciated, such as the low ceiling in the isolation loose box, easily banged by a horse tossing its head; or the narrow doors between the forage barn and the stable block designed to knock a bale of hay or straw out of your hands! Overall the facility was a big improvement on the previous accommodation, and the availability of training and exercise areas was greatly appreciated.

At 11.30 am on 19th October 1971 the building was officially opened in a ceremony performed by the Master of the Queen's Horse, His Grace The Duke of Beaufort, in company with the Lord Mayor Alderman Mrs Helen Bloom, Chairman of the Watch Committee Alderman Marcus Hartnell, the Chief Constable Mr. George Twist, and other visiting dignitaries. The Duke unveiled a plaque on the wall near

*The Duke of Beaufort at the opening of the new stables, with Chief Inspector Cheetham
(centre) and Inspector Langley*

the main gateway before inspecting representatives of the two Sections
introduced by Chief Inspector Cheetham and Inspector Langley. The
guests then toured the building before returning to Kingsweston House
where a buffet lunch had been prepared. The brochure for the opening
ceremony gives a brief history of the Mounted Section (although it
incorrectly states its foundation date as 1889) and lists the Mounted
personnel as 1 Chief Inspector; 2 Sergeants; and 16 Constables. There
were 12 horses at this time, and the accommodation provided for
them in the stable block consisted of 4 loose boxes and 8 stalls,
together with a separate isolation loose box across the yard from the
main block. Ken Bush had been the only Sergeant on the unit since
he had taken over from Frank Turner in 1969, but he was now joined
in the supervisory capacity by Frank Knight who was promoted to
Sergeant about the time the unit moved to Bower Ashton. The entire
unit was now centralised under one roof for the first time in its history.

In November police horse *Clifton*, which had been purchased in
1964 and was now 12 years old, had developed respiratory problems, which made him unsuitable for further police work. It was
decided to retire *Clifton* to the rented ground in Ashton Court,
where the civilian groom or the mounted officers could keep an eye
on him. *Clifton* survived in placid retirement in the paddock at
Ashton Court until his death in 1981. He was replaced by a 4-year-
old bay gelding bought from Jack James for £450. The horse was
reported at the time to have a "very good temperament", and it

was decided to name him *Ashton*, after the unit's new headquarters.

Up until this time the ceremonial helmet of each mounted escort was crowned with a silver ball, but for some time it had been desired to enhance the uniform with a plume, after the fashion of the Royal Horse Guards. The plumes themselves were a modest enough investment and it was agreed that they should be purchased and brought into use after the opening of Bower Ashton. The first ceremonial escort on which they were employed was the Remembrance Sunday escort of the Lord Mayor to the Cenotaph in Bristol's city centre. The officer in charge, Chief Inspector Cheetham, wore a red plume, while the escorts wore white. They presented a very impressive display at an event which traditionally attracted a large gathering of citizens, and from that day the plumes have been used as part of the ceremonial uniform to enhance the dignified image of the escorts.

In pre-Bower Ashton days the mounted officers worked either an early shift (usually commencing at 5.45am), a day shift (commencing at 9am), or a split shift which entailed returning to the stables after a

Mounted escort with white plumes at St Mary Redcliffe on Rush Sunday

PC Hurst riding Ashton on patrol in Corn St

period of time off in order to check on the horses and provide them with fresh water and hay to last them through the night. The mounted officers were rarely required to work nights unless a police operation demanded it, so the police night staff at Redland, St.George and Bedminster had the additional duty of checking the police horses at some stage during the night. Because the stables adjoined the police stations, this presented no problem and the security risk was minimal. However this was not so easy at Bower Ashton, situated as it was in an isolated and unlit area outside the city. The problem was overcome by nominating one mounted officer each week to perform night duty at the stables in order to attend to the animals' needs and provide a police presence for security reasons. As the heavy work in any stable is done first thing in the morning when the horses are "mucked-out", the majority of the remaining officers available worked from 5.45am, with others covering a day shift or an afternoon and evening shift. The system adopted seemed to work well, with the strength appropriately placed during the day to perform the necessary stable duties and to be available for police operations. The officers were assisted by the employment of full-time civilian grooms who worked during the day to put down bedding, feed the horses and manage the general day-to-day running of the stables.

The city of Bristol was divided into 17 patrol areas, most of which could be managed from Bower Ashton on a three or four-hour patrol. Some were designated as box patrols when the mounted units were dropped off at pre-arranged locations to cover the district before riding back to Bower Ashton. The patrol number, Division of patrol and the boundary of the patrol were printed onto cards, which were issued to the mounted officers by the Sergeant each day.

The drop-off point for the box patrols included Kingsweston Police Station, Brislington Trading Estate, Monks Park Avenue and Thicket Avenue. Patrol Area 1 included the Downs, which involved a ride across the Clifton Suspension Bridge, and Patrol Area 2 was an exercise route, which included the tow-path alongside the River Avon and the Ashton Court Estate. This latter area was often used to settle a lively horse or to educate a young one (called a "remount" - an old Army term). The advantages of the Ashton Court location, with the proximity of the city on one hand and the countryside on the other, were thereby utilised to the full.

During 1972 the Musical Ride displays continued with performances at the North Somerset Show Ashton Court and in the main arena at the Royal Bath and West Show, Shepton Mallet. The events were very well received by both show authorities and public alike. In addition competition success continued, with *Avon* ridden by PC Grace, and *Kingsweston* ridden by PC Marment (who had transferred from *St.Michael*) entered for the South of England Show at Ardingly, Sussex. In the competition for the **Horace Smith Cup**, *Avon* was placed 1st and *Kingsweston* 2nd. In the **King George V Cup** open to all police forces, *Kingsweston* was placed 2nd and *Avon* was 3rd. Finally at the Liverpool Police Horse Show two weeks later, the Bristol horses became champions again by being placed 1st in the Pairs Competition, and at the end of the Show, the Liverpool Watch Committee's Challenge Cup was presented to *Kingsweston* and PC Jim Marment for having gained the highest number of points.

L to R: PC Marment on St Michael; Sgt Bush; PC Grace on Avon

During the autumn two more requests were received by the Chief Constable for the Mounted Branch to give displays. The Abergavenny and Border Counties Show asked for the Branch to perform the musical quadrille and tent-pegging display at the Show which was scheduled for the following July, 1973. The Dairy Festival at Weston-super-Mare, which had employed the horses the previous year also requested a repeat performance at their next Show in June. Both applications were approved by the Watch Committee on payment of the appropriate charges.

PC Milsom tent-pegging on Prince

Tent-pegging was a mounted sporting activity still carried on by the Army and some of the police mounted establishments around the country. History has it that this skill, which entailed galloping along a straight line and removing a piece of wood from the ground using a lance, was developed by the British Army in India during the last century as a way of maintaining the combat fitness of horses and riders during times of military inactivity. The sport grew in popularity when transferred to England, and competitions were held between the various cavalry regiments for the honour of being "Tent-pegging Champion". As the mounted regiments disappeared, the sport faded but was maintained as a class at Horse Shows as a method of training and instilling boldness in the horse and rider. And it was a lot of fun!

However, the Bristol unit, under a policy adopted by Inspector Bradley, had never seriously attempted to win the tent-pegging or skill-at-arms classes at the shows, preferring to stick to the Best Trained class. It was argued that this category demonstrated all the best attributes required of a police horse when going about its duties. However the sport was practised occasionally on the mounted training days, when it was considered beneficial to "stretch the horses legs and give them a blow" after a period of contained schoolwork.

On one memorable occasion during the late '60s, Inspector Peters had agreed to let PC Alan Milsom ride his horse *Prince* in a tent-pegging class at the Liverpool Horse Show, and they had travelled up with the Best Trained team specifically to enter the class. Training runs had gone well, but when the time came to enter the arena for the contest itself, *Prince* refused to go anywhere near the gate and was thus disqualified without even running! After this enlightening experience, it was decided to leave the sporting classes to others! But the event was none-the-less exciting to watch, and it was maintained by the Bristol branch as an element of their riding displays.

The following year the Chief Constable reported that he had received an application from the promoters of the Bath Searchlight Tattoo for the services of the display team of the Mounted Branch together with the Motor-cycling Section who had been trained for display purposes. He said that the Tattoo was being presented on a considerable scale, including over 500 troops from the three Armed Services, and any profits would be applied to the Armed Services charities. The Tattoo would be held daily from Tuesday 12th to Saturday 16th June. The recommendation was approved in view of the high-profile and professional nature of the event, on condition of a charge of £100 per day being made to cover all expenses.

Training with the motor-cyclists in Royal Victoria Park, Bath

Training began, together with police motor-cyclists, to prepare a display commensurate with the usual high quality entertainment provided by the Armed Services. The display was devised, with assistance from the Mounted Section, by Sgt Clarence Hudson of the Traffic Department and became one of the highlights of the Tattoo. The event took place in the Royal Victoria Park in Bath, and in addition to the choreography of movement between the horses and motor-cycles, a tent-pegging contest was held between the two Sections, with a pillion passenger carrying the lance for the motor-cyclists. This proved to be extremely popular with the audiences, and the display was revived later as one of the main attractions in the arena at the Royal Bath and West Show.

Sadly, despite its popularity with the public, stringent police spending constraints ended the show career of the motor-cycle section, and the display team was disbanded in 1974. The Mounted Section continued with their limited number of Musical Ride displays, including one at Stratford Park, Stroud in July, but they were performed without the spectacular addition of the motor-cyclists and their machines.

1973 also saw the retirement of a former show winner, police horse *St.Michael*. A replacement was purchased for the sum of £625. Then in September a road accident created another unwanted vacancy on the Branch. At 8pm on 18th September PC Gary White was riding his horse *Justice* along Clanage Road towards the stables. He was returning from a football match at Ashton Gate and had left the well-lit area of the Cumberland Basin and entered the darkness of Clanage Road, when the horse was struck from behind by a Ford Anglia car being driven by a woman who had failed to see it. PC White and the passengers in the car were taken to the Bristol Royal Infirmary with injuries, which fortunately were of a minor nature, but *Justice* had broken both his back legs and had to be put down on the spot by the Veterinary Surgeon who attended the scene.

The subsequent report indicated that a light was displayed on the offside stirrup as required, but a number of cars were parked on the nearside of Clanage Road without lights, and this had meant that PC White was further into the road than would normally have been the case. It was later suggested that the riders should be equipped with fluorescent jackets similar to those used by police motor-cyclists, and the Chief Constable agreed to look into this suggestion. From that time any night patrols were performed with the officers wearing reflective jackets and the horses wearing reflective spats around their lower legs in addition to the lights slung under the stirrups. Whenever dog vans were available, they were detailed to position themselves behind the mounted troop in Clanage Road until they had reached the Cumberland Basin on an outward journey, or the stables on an inward journey. As a result of these precautions, no more accidents occurred along Clanage Road in spite of the innumerable times it has been used by police horses since *Justice* was killed.

The Horse of the Year Show in 1973 brought Bristol's first success in the competition since *Redcliffe* had won six years earlier. Police horse *Avon* ridden by PC Joe Grace was awarded the title Police Horse of the Year when he won the Best Trained class at Wembley. The title crowned another remarkable record for the Bristol branch in the showing field as *Avon* had already won 15 other events around the country during his career thus far, and there was more to come as the horse was still in his prime.

Mounted officers on duty near Eastville Stadium, mid-70s

Police horses continued to attend all Bristol City and Bristol Rovers home matches at Ashton Gate and Eastville respectively. The proximity of City's ground was an undoubted bonus, but Eastville Stadium required either the use of the horsebox or the necessity of the best part of an hour's ride across the city to attend

Sgt Bush on Kingsweston at Ashton Gate

games. Most of the events passed off peacefully, but every now and then disorder occurred between rival fans, and the horses were used to separate and move along the opposing factions. Police intelligence on the various clubs improved until it was possible to predict which fixtures were likely to cause trouble, and plans were prepared accordingly. Rival supporters had to be separated inside the grounds and the visiting fans were often shepherded along *en masse* from the nearest railway station or coach park.

In 1973 one of the biggest clubs in the country, Manchester United, had been relegated from the First to the Second Division of the Football League, but they nevertheless maintained a following of many thousands of fans for their away trips. When they visited Ashton Gate for the fixture with Bristol City, sporadic outbreaks of violence kept the mounted units and foot police busy, but they were unable to prevent damage being caused to car aerials and windscreen wipers, and many front windows were smashed in the houses along Coronation Road.

On 1st April 1974 the Bristol Constabulary ceased to exist as a separate force, and was amalgamated into the new Avon and Somerset Constabulary. This consisted of the new county of Avon (including the city of Bristol and the southern area of Gloucestershire) and the reduced county of Somerset. Mr George Twist resigned his post as Chief Constable and was subsequently appointed to become one of Her Majesty's Inspectors of Constabulary. Mr. Kenneth Steele, who had been Chief Constable of the Somerset and Bath Constabulary, was confirmed as Chief Constable of the new Force. The

Kenneth Steele

Mounted Branch would from henceforth have to be prepared for their "beat" to be of one of the largest in the country in terms of acreage. It included Weston-super-Mare with its huge summer population, the Badminton Horse Trials, the Royal Bath and West Show and the Somerset Winter Carnivals, which attracted thousands of spectators every year. All these additional duties were to be performed over the ensuing months and would represent a very steep learning curve for the officers and horses as they faced situations new to the unit which had previously been predominantly city-based.

Around this time of amalgamation there were further rumblings of threat concerning the Mounted Section, when it was feared that the new Chief Constable Kenneth Steele did not support the maintenance of such a unit in his Force. This did not subsequently prove to be the case, but at a time of great change it was unsettling to hear the rumour, which seemed to take on an impetus of its own, as these things often do. In fact Kenneth Steele was later to give his name to one of the most successful show horses the Force ever owned, and during his time in charge was never less than supportive of the group.

The Mounted Branch became fully aware of their change of circumstances in November 1974, when they were required to send 6 horses to Weston-super-Mare to help supervise the enormous crowds which filled the town to watch the famous illuminated Winter Carnival go by. The plan was to place two mounted officers near the start of the procession, two about halfway along the route and two near the end, with the intention of keeping an eye on the crowd to prevent any accidents and ensure a clear route as the floats went by. Unfortunately for the horses, which had never seen an illuminated carnival before, the first float was a 15 feet-high giant leopard, poised in mid-spring with mouth agape and white teeth gleaming! To the equine

The leading float of the 1974 Weston-super-Mare Carnival!

brain the papier-mache monster was a distinct threat. In spite of the best efforts of their riders, the first two horses made good their escape by continuing along the road in a less than dignified rush. They were brought to a halt when they reached their two colleagues at the half-way point, but when the "monster" appeared round the corner, all four horses decided that discretion was the better part of valour and took off again in search of safer locations. Eventually all six horses arrived back at the horsebox in a cloud of steam, convinced that they had just outrun the jaws of hell! Since those days better planning and more gradual exposure to the operation has resulted in the police horses leading the Carnivals all over the Somerset circuit, without further mishap.

In January 1975 three new officers began an Initial Equitation Course at Bower Ashton with instructor Sgt Frank Knight. The officers were PC Derek Gatehouse, PC Tim Liddeatt and myself. We were to fill vacancies caused by the retirement of three older members, including that of PC Joe Grace. He had the misfortune to break his leg in a riding accident while off duty and was retired on a medical pension. During the ensuing months PC Alan Milsom also retired and took up the business of saddler in Shirehampton - which he still successfully pursues. Other personnel changes about this time included the medical retirement of Sgt. Ken Bush who succumbed to an injury to his knee sustained while riding, and the installation of his replacement, Gerry Haskey, who was promoted to Sergeant on transfer from the West Midlands Constabulary. PC David Young and PC David Gibbons also joined the group during the summer.

The Public Order training days continued to be held at the Army Apprentices College in Chepstow, and the horses and riders were becoming used to the manoeuvres required in the face of a rioting crowd supplied by the enthusiastic apprentices. On one occasion though, the visit was not so welcome when police horse *Cumberland*, still excited by the exercise, escaped from his rider whilst being unsaddled and galloped across the Camp Commandant's immaculately kept front lawn! As the divots went flying one could imagine the generations of young soldiers who had tended the bowling-green surface being less than pleased with the resultant scars which probably took months to repair!

One of my first experiences of the effectiveness of police horses occurred during the following football season, when the local derby game brought the Rovers to Ashton Gate. As usual, the match attracted a full house and, again as usual, most of the fans enjoyed the rivalry without recourse to mindless posturing or violence. As the fans left after the game however, a confrontation flared between several hundred opposing supporters at the end of Clift House Road. I was in that area riding *Redcliffe* in company with Sgt Frank Knight who rode *Brunel*. We positioned ourselves between the factions and moved back and forth keeping them apart until assistance arrived and the crowd dispersed. It was a simple exercise for the horses, but one that prevented the situation from escalating into something much more serious.

During the summer of 1976 an exercise was arranged for the Mounted Branch by the senior officers of the Support Services Division, with the objective of ascertaining whether mounted officers could assist in searching for missing persons over rural and open countryside. Apart from one or two isolated incidents the unit had never been used for such operations, and it was hoped that the combined advantages of horses' ability to manoeuvre over rough land, the extra height and vision of the riders to look over hedges and down into rhines, and the amount of ground the horse was able to cover, would all prove invaluable when searching for missing persons. And so it proved. The exercise took place over the rolling Mendip Hills. Stuffed dummies were placed in a variety of awkward and hidden locations, and the mounted officers swept the area in pairs, locating all the dummies within hours.

Four mounted officers on a search for a missing person

As a final test, a dummy was placed in a spot where the dead body of a woman had lain undiscovered for several months in an incident two years earlier. The horses engaged on the exercise formed a wide line, with the riders just keeping each other in view. Crook Peak provided a dramatic backdrop as they began to sweep back across the hills. Within 30 minutes the remaining dummy was located, and the Section had convinced the senior officers of their abilities in searching situations. From this time the unit received regular calls from all over the Force area and beyond to attend as an initial or additional response in "misper" searches.

Later in the year, the police at Wellington in the south of Somerset, requested the assistance of the unit in a search for Julie Sydenham, a three-year-old girl believed murdered and hidden on rough and common land nearby. Although large tracts of land had already been searched by officers on foot, assisted by the police dog section and aided by dozens of volunteers, the body had not been found. Six officers and horses were sent from Bristol and after searching the common land for two hours, PC Philip Jones, who was riding *Bristowe*, and Sgt Gerry Haskey, riding *Kingsweston*, discovered the body in a plastic bag stuffed underneath a bush. As a result the tragic case was brought to a conclusion with the arrest and eventual conviction of the murderer. The horses were also utilised about this time by the Devon and Cornwall Constabulary who were trying to locate the body of another unfortunate girl, Genette Tate. In spite of all efforts however, the body was never recovered, and the whereabouts remains a mystery to this day.

Another more pleasant duty that became a regular requirement of the unit was the attendance for a few hours of horse and rider at various schools in the Force area, to back up the police schools liaison team. The team usually became resident at a school for a week, teaching the children about the police service and its role in society. They also made the most of the opportunity to express the importance of accident and crime prevention. But inevitably the highlight of the week for most of the children was the appearance in their playground of a police horse. It was possible to talk to the children from the horse's back about the duties of the Mounted Section, and later to put the animal through its paces, with demonstrations of walk, trot and canter, if on grass, and an exhibition of the lateral movements so valuable to police horses. To watch the children's faces as an enormous horse moved sideways towards them and then stop within inches of their toes made the exercise well worthwhile! They were also able to let off steam when they were provided with flags, banners, rattles and drums and became a "nuisance lane" for the horse to negotiate. In addition to being great fun for the children, it was a useful exercise for the horses, especially if young and inexperienced, in facing such a din in that type of controlled situation.

PC Foulkes riding Redcliffe on a school visit 1976

Many years after I joined the unit, I had the pleasant experience of young adults coming up to me while I was on patrol and relating, with some glee, their distant memory of the police horse visit to their school whilst they were children. Whatever else they may have forgotten this memory remained with them.

The Horse of the Year Show of 1976 produced an unexpected winner in police horse *Ashton*. The horse had never appeared to fulfil its potential since joining the Section in 1971, but during the year PC Tony Clarke became responsible for its training and then rode the horse to a memorable victory. It would be true to say that *Ashton* was never going to be one of Bristol's great horses, but with Tony Clarke making up in expertise what the animal lacked in talent, the final prize of the year was won - much to the surprise of a lot of people!

1977 provided a historic landmark for the Mounted Branch. The year was a celebration of the 25th year of the accession of Queen Elizabeth II - the Silver Jubilee - and the Queen toured the nation,

Bristol City Centre 1977. Silver Jubilee mounted escort for Queen Elizabeth II;
Chief Inspector Cheetham on Brandon on right of royal carriage

with thousands turning out all over the country to join in the cele-brations. The Queen and Duke of Edinburgh came to Bristol in August, and had, before the visit, granted permission to the Constabulary for the local Mounted Police to provide Her Majesty with a ceremonial escort for part of the tour. Normally the Household Cavalry would have provided this, but it was known that Bristol maintained the tradition of mounted escorts, and thus the honour was accorded to the unit who became the only police Mounted Section to have escorted a reigning sovereign. The day before the escort took place, Bower Ashton became the temporary home for the Queen's horses and carriage, and the mounted unit was transferred to the Lord Mayor's stables in Ashton Court to prepare for the event.

Chief Inspector Richard Cheetham was officer-in-charge of the escort as outrider on police horse *Brandon*, with Sgt Frank Knight, riding *Brunel*, leading on the offside of the front half-section. I was fortunate enough to be in position right behind the Queen's car-riage on *Redcliffe* and probably had the best view of the entire proceedings. We collected the royal party at the Bridgehead on the City Centre and began the escort through Queen Square to Temple Meads, where they were to board the royal train. The procession was cheered every yard of the way, with children often running up to the carriage (no doubt to the consternation of those concerned with security!) to present posies of flowers to the Queen, which she always graciously accepted. It was a memorable and historic occasion for the Mounted Branch who were honoured to have such royal recognition for one of their traditional roles.

The same year the Section took part in another high-profile escort, when they combined with the Royal Canadian Mounted Police (on tour in the UK and giving displays at the Royal Bath and West Show) in an escort for the Lord Mayor of Bristol through the city on a weekday. Normally the ceremonial escorts take place on Sunday mornings, which limits the size of the crowds looking on (except for Remembrance Sunday) so the arrival of the colourful entourage in Broadmead created quite a stir.

About this time the Section took possession of a young horse which had been the subject of a competition amongst local school-children who were asked to choose a suitable name. The winning entry was "*Centaur*", the name of the mythical beast which was half-man, half-horse, because, as the young girl said who won the competition, "a policeman and his horse are as one". Although *Centaur* never achieved the cult status of *Robin* or *Redcliffe*, he was certainly one of the Section's best-ever horses who took to the work like a duck to water and soon proved himself to be (as they say in the trade) practically bomb-proof! The strength of the Section was now increased to thirteen horses, taking into account the non-operational remount undergoing its training. Another new recruit took to the stage at the Badminton event in this year, and he was named *Jubilee* by Prince Andrew. This horse was not to enjoy the lengthy career achieved by *Centaur*, and after a few years of competent service he succumbed to a brain haemorrhage and died, ironically, while on duty at the Badminton Horse Trials.

In October 1977 six officers and horses of the Mounted Section were required to attend at Home Park, Plymouth, the home of Plymouth Argyle FC, as the venue had been selected for the European Cup match between Manchester United and St. Etienne of France. The tie was actually a home game for the Manchester club but due to crowd disturbances at Old Trafford on previous occasions, they were ordered to play the game outside a 200-mile radius of Manchester, and Plymouth's ground was selected. The ground is ideally situated for horse patrol work, set as it is in park-land, and although the game attracted a capacity crowd there were no disturbances among the fans - perhaps due partly to the high-profile policing, and to the fact that Manchester United won 2-0 and qualified for the next round! It was a very long day for the Bristol horses, but the operation was counted a success and result-ed in further excursions to Home Park in later seasons, when the home club hosted other potentially difficult matches.

The usual Musical Ride display was given a different perspective in May 1978, when a combined Mounted and Dog display formed the main attraction of a Bower Ashton Open Day. Thousands came to view the premises and to take advantage of the opportunity to get near the animals in their homebase. The novel display proved to be quite attractive and gave the Sections a chance to show off the training and discipline of both units.

The 1978 showing season provided some memorable moments. *Avon*, ridden by PC Paul Bernard, won the Best Trained Police Horse class at the South of England Show, with PC Alan Jobbins second on *Centaur*. The latter pair also won the Best Turned Out com-petition. At the Metropolitan Police Horse Show at Imber Court *Kingsweston*, ridden by PC Jim Marment, won both the Provincial and Championship classes, with *Avon* (PC Paul Bernard) second in both events. These positions were reversed in the Provincial

PC Bernard on Avon

class of the City of Birmingham Police Horse Show, but the Championship went once again to *Kingsweston*. PC Philip Jones riding *Somerset* also competed in this show in the Best Turned Out class (3rd) and he managed a creditable 3rd place in the Tent-pegging contest against 25 other competitors. Later in the year *Kingsweston* and *Avon* won the Pairs competition at the Horse of the Year Show to bring the season to a suitable conclusion.

The year also saw the institution of the Force Internal Competition for Mounted officers, which was the idea of the Horsemaster, Dick Cheetham. The intention was to provide everyone on the unit with an incentive and opportunity to show what they could do in a competitive atmosphere, and the motivation to bring the kit, horse and training up to a good standard. Chief Inspector Cheetham donated a magnificent **"Horsemaster's Trophy"** to be presented to the winning rider in the Dressage and Street Nuisance phase; and the Chairman of the Police Authority, Mr Ian Crawford, contributed the **"Crawford Trophy"**, awarded to the Best Turned Out officer and mount. The current showing team was excluded from the contest, but the standard of the first "Internal", held at Bower Ashton, was high and was eventually won by PC Alan Jobbins riding *Centaur*. The competition was deemed to be a success and was held

Lambourn six-horsebox

annually from that time, with the dressage and nuisance phases staged in the grounds at Kingsweston House, until 1994 when several such "non-operational" activities were abandoned.

1979 eventually saw the end of the horse trailer that had caused such consternation among the Section's drivers when it had made its appearance in 1956. A Lambourn rigid body horsebox capable of carrying six horses in echelon formation and including a large passenger area and adjoining tack room replaced it. Some of the unit's larger horses were beginning to object strongly to the tight fit of the trailer and, as the new box could now provide the convenience of changing facilities, the vehicle was certainly overdue, and it looked very smart in its fresh blue livery. At last the Avon and Somerset horses could be efficiently moved around the Force area, and would no longer look like the poor relations when parked alongside the gleaming horseboxes of other Constabularies at the Shows.

The Chief Constable Kenneth Steele CBE, KPM retired from the Force in 1979 and one of his last acts as Chief was to name the Mounted Section's new horse, which he called *Steele*. The horse was being trained by

Brian Weigh

PC Tony Clarke who had already achieved remarkable success with remounts in the past. Mr Steele had selected the right horse to perpetuate his name as the animal became one of the most prolific show winners the Force had owned. Kenneth Steele was succeeded as Chief Constable by Mr Brian Weigh who had formerly been an Assistant Chief Constable in the Somerset and Bath Constabulary.

PC Tim Liddeatt wearing the new riding helmet

1979 was also the retirement year of police horse *Redcliffe* who had been such a good servant to the Force. In his younger days he had been a champion animal and he retained his courage and boldness right to the end of his service. He was retired to a farm near Yate Rocks and saw out his days there in some comfort. He was replaced by a young horse which was called *Mendip*, the name having been selected to obviate the criticism of a north-of-Force bias! Sadly, however, within a year *Mendip* developed a chronic lameness, and he eventually had to be put down.

The headwear adopted by the unit just after the War - the flat cap - was now superseded by a hard helmet in the style of a jockey cap. Apart from the obvious safety considerations it was considered necessary to set a good example to riders from other walks of life, and in so doing appeased the British Horse Society and other official equine bodies which had been agitating for such a move for some time.

WPC Diana Day being welcomed by police horse George II

At the end of the Seventies, Chief Inspector Cheetham suffered serious heart problems and was off sick for many months. He underwent heart surgery and recovered at the Police Convalescent Home at Hove, but the operation appeared to be a success and he was able to resume his duties as the 1980s dawned. The new decade also witnessed the end of eighty-one years of the Mounted Section being an exclusively male domain, as WPC Diana Day (later Davies) was accepted as a full member of the unit following her successful initial course. The larger Mounted Sections of the country - notably the Metropolitan Police - had for some years been employing female officers, so the move was not a great surprise, and Diana proved herself to be a competent rider who fully deserved her place on the Branch.

Sgt Frank Knight

During August 1980 Sgt Frank Knight retired from the Mounted Section he had joined 28 years previously, and the position was filled by the promotion of Alan Jobbins. Alan had demonstrated a riding and training talent far above the average, and his ability to communicate with his pupils and willingness to pass on his knowledge had been put to good use by the Section. The position as Sergeant now gave him official authority to continue with the training work, and the promotion was a popular one.

Other moves on the Section involved horse reallocations. PC Paul Bernard was allocated the young horse *Jubilee*, and PC Gary White was transferred from *Cumberland* to *Avon*. He was able to achieve immediate success when he registered a 2nd place in the Provincial and Championship classes at the South of England Show at

Sgt Alan Jobbins

Ardingly. Not surprisingly, the champion was stablemate *Kingsweston*, again ridden by Jim Marment. The Birmingham Horse Show ended with *Kingsweston* winning the Best Trained class for Forces outside the West Midlands, but *Avon* and Gary White managed to pip them to the Open Championship. The Branch's winning reputation, now established for over twenty years, showed no sign of diminishing.

As the century entered its eighth decade, the problem of the football hooligan was another and less welcome facet of Mounted Branch life which also showed no sign of diminishing. If anything, the situation was getting worse. Nearly every match bubbled with some disorder. Fans had to be carefully segregated, both in transit to and from the game and whilst in the stadium. Running fights became the norm in Ashton Road and Stapleton Road on such occasions, and the horses' mobility often came into its own as they broke up gangs or defused volatile situations. On one occasion rioting Chelsea fans intent on facing up to the opposition nearly broke onto the pitch at Eastville through a large hole in the perimeter fence; the actions of the horses prevented this happening and forced the offenders back into their appointed areas. Another time a large group of Arsenal fans invaded Greville Smythe Park after a game to get at Bristol City fans. Without the prompt action of the police horses on the scene in

Escorting football supporters in Stapleton Road, Eastville

breaking up the fighting groups and interposing themselves to prevent repetition, the situation might well have developed into a full-scale riot with potentially serious consequences. It was apparent that the problem was a long-term one and coupled with the Section's other duties of searching, patrol and escort, seemed to indicate that the years ahead were going to be a busy time for the Mounted Section.

CHAPTER EIGHT

THE EIGHTIES

The district of St Pauls, in Bristol's inner city, sprang to national prominence during 1980 as a result of a full scale riot which lasted for many hours and resulted in thousands of pounds worth of damage being caused and considerable arson and looting taking place. The situation had escalated from a police raid on the Black and White Cafe in St Pauls which was launched in an effort to apprehend the drug dealers which had blighted the area. The response from the local criminal fraternity caught the police by surprise, and the ensuing riot found them ill prepared to contain it. Eventually the Chief Constable Brian Weigh (having to make an unenviable decision on the spot which was later much criticised) decided to withdraw his officers in an effort to defuse the situation. When off-duty mounted officers heard of the riot, many rang through to Bower Ashton with offers of help, but the official call for assistance never came.

The Bristol police horses were not utilised at the scene for reasons best known to the senior officers in charge. It was a matter of some disgruntlement that the unit had not been employed. It is possible that the senior officers thought that in its early stages, the riot could be subdued without the use of police horses which may have exposed them to accusations of heavy-handedness and insensitivity. By the time the option was reconsidered, however, the situation had escalated beyond the capability of the Mounted Branch, as the police had temporarily abandoned the area. Order was only eventually restored when a small army of police officers from surrounding forces arrived and together with their local colleagues brought the rule of law back to the stricken area.

It is easy with hindsight to point to measures that might have contained the riot more successfully, but decisions had to be made under the most arduous circumstances. However, valuable lessons were learned because of this incident (which later paled in comparison with street riots in Brixton, Toxteth and other parts of the country). As a result, plans were formulated for a more efficient police response and for the acquisition of protective equipment for police officers, should the situation recur.

St Pauls became a sensitive district for a long time after the riots and, several months later when a similar episode appeared to be brewing, the Mounted Section received a call to stand by in case they were needed. Six horses and officers were loaded into the horsebox and maintained a watch for several hours on the outskirts of the area. Fortunately the situation resolved itself, and the unit later returned to Bower Ashton without having been deployed.

Following the success of the Mounted and Dog Sections combined display which took place at the Bower Ashton Open Day, another three performances were given during 1981 to enhance the profile of the units and boost public relations. The displays were given at the Flowerdown Fair which took place at RAF Locking near Weston-super-Mare, at Taunton Racecourse and at Bridgend

PC Wilson on Mayfield patrolling the Sea Front at Weston-super-Mare, mid-70s

as part of a South Wales Police Open Day. The Mounted Section had already given independent displays at Flowerdown Fair in previous years, which had always been well-received, but on one occasion the combination of horses and aircraft caused consternation when a Vulcan bomber flew low over the arena, generating some excitement amongst the animals and more than a little discomfiture for their riders!

Some of the hard-pressed divisions of the Force were beginning to realise the potential of the Mounted Section. Minehead police, in the far west of Somerset, had an adequate strength for most of the year, but the summer influx of visitors meant that they were often stretched over the holiday period - not unlike Weston-super-Mare, which had been utilising the horses during the summer for some years. Consequently, arrangements were made for two officers and horses to spend several days at a time patrolling the town, sea front and popular areas of neighbouring Exmoor to assist the local police in their cover. The high-profile nature of the mounted patrols was very well received by both locals and holidaymakers alike, and functions such as the Dunster Country Fair also received a visit from the horses. This was very popular amongst what was a horse-minded community. The patrols continued all that summer when priority duties permitted, and the public relations boost was a bonus to the practical assistance the mounted units were able to provide for the local police. In addition to patrols such as these, mounted officers also attended events such as Bath Races, held at Lansdown, and the Royal Bath and West Show at Shepton Mallet, where their ability to patrol through the packed thoroughfares of the showground and around the perimeter car parks made their attendance highly desirable.

The 1981 showing season marked the first national success for *Steele*. The year had also been a successful one for *Avon* ridden by PC Gary White, and although the old horse was now nearing the end of his career, he won the Best Trained class at the Royal Windsor Show, the Best Trained (Provincial) and Reserve Championship at the South of England Show at Ardingly, and the Best Trained (Provincial) at Birmingham. In the latter event *Steele* ridden by PC Tony Clarke came 3rd; but he became a champion for the first time by winning the Championship at the same Show. Another first came in the shape of the Tent-pegging trophy at the

Metropolitan Police Horse Show, carried off by PC Philip Jones on the very quick horse *Somerset*. Although tent-pegging was still considered by the Bristol unit to be very much a secondary event, it seemed that they possessed the talent to compete with the cream of the Met - and on their own ground!

The Horse of the Year Show 1981 provided the evidence that *Steele's* win earlier in the season had been no lucky fluke. Although still comparatively inexperienced, the horse ridden by PC Tony Clarke became **Police Horse of the Year** for the first time; and there began a sequence of wins at the Show which eventually was to place him, in police horse circles at least, in the *Red Rum* category of legend. But this was all in the future, and on this occasion *Avon* (Gary White) was placed second behind *Steele*, completing a memorable weekend for the Avon and Somerset stable.

PC Clarke on Steele collecting the trophy at the Horse of the Year Show

In addition to support provided to the outposts of the Force, the mounted unit was frequently called upon to reinforce the busy Central Division, with patrols into the Broadmead shopping precinct and surrounding area. If the mounted officer stopped to perform observations, he often found himself surrounded by shoppers and children, who were attracted to the police horse like filings to a magnet. Invariably on these occasions the same three questions would be fired at the officer - "What's his name?" "How old is he?" and "How big is he?" No matter how many times the same questions had to be answered, the officer had to remember that it was a first-time genuine query, and the rapport provided by the animal had to be reinforced by courteous replies from the rider!

Sometimes assistance was given in the apprehension of shoplifters in the area (on one occasion the culprit gave himself up when he heard galloping hooves coming up behind him!), and lost children and lost and found property were also regularly dealt with. The area patrols continued throughout the year but were particularly reinforced during the run-up to Christmas and during the January sales. In the early days of these patrols, large gangs of youths used to gather outside one of the record shops in Broadmead with the intention of rushing up and down, pushing shoppers over and generally disturbing the peace of the area. After meeting the police horses on a couple of occasions the gangs were made to see the error of their ways, and the problem stopped. Half a ton of horseflesh, they must have realised, could push far more effectively than they could themselves!

During the early months of 1982 the Bedford lorry, which had been purchased thirteen years earlier as the Section's first proper horsebox, was replaced by a Dodge vehicle capable of carrying 4 horses. The new horsebox boasted a living area and kitchen which, although small, was a big improvement when compared with the total lack of crew facilities in the Bedford.

Police horse Sulis

Police Support training (as riot training was euphemistically called), which had started with the visits to the Army Apprentices College, now took on a more formal and professional edge. The lessons of St Pauls had been well learned, and the Mounted Section now participated regularly with properly equipped foot officers in a variety of manoeuvres that contributed to efficient defensive and offensive tactics. The venues for such training changed to new locations around the Force area as the Divisions supplied officers for the training, and the horseboxes could frequently be seen travelling the motorway and main roads to Bath, Weston-super-Mare and Taunton as the horses played their full part. The use of the fully protective NATO style helmet, together with body armour for the officers and horses, was not far off.

The summer of 1982 witnessed the arrival at the stable of a new police horse which was named *Sulis* by the Mayor of Bath. The horse was of a different stamp to those usually recruited to the Section, in that he looked more like a racehorse! *Sulis* soon demonstrated a turn of speed and certain unpredictability which went with his appearance. He showed every confidence in road work and on patrol, but his less engaging habit of biting and kicking anyone within range very quickly made the establishment realise that they had taken on board yet another character!

The autumn and early winter of 1982 provided the Section with two memorable events. *Steele* (PC Tony Clarke) won his second and consecutive Police Horse of the Year title and PC Jim Marment retired from the Constabulary, having completed 32 years service, 27 years of which had been with the Mounted Section. He continued winning throughout his last showing season on police horse *Kingsweston* and, once Jim had retired, the horse was reallocated to PC Dave Young. Jim's place on the group was taken by the unit's second female member, WPC Sue Blanchard. Another newcomer at this time was a remount which was named *Woodspring* by the Mayor of Weston-super-Mare. The horse, in partnership with PC Tim Liddeatt, was later to have much success in the sporting classes of the Horse Shows.

PC Marment on Kingsweston

During the summer of 1983 the Section received a call for assistance from the Chief Constable of the Dorset and Bournemouth Constabulary. The beaches and dunes of the Studland Bay area on the south coast were famed as nudist resorts, but its reputation had also attracted people who were committing indecency offences while masquerading as legitimate nudists. The local police had difficulty in apprehending these offenders because of the terrain. There was some competition on the Section to volunteer for the job, but subsequently PC David Hurst on *Avon* and PC John Burgess on *Bristol* were despatched to spend the weekend patrolling the dunes and sands. The idea was to discourage offenders from infiltrating the area and to reassure the law-abiding naturist that their complaints were being taken seriously! The excursion was entirely successful and led in later years to patrols of the beach and dunes near Burnham-on-Sea when similar offences were being committed there.

During the year the Chief Constable Brian Weigh retired from the Force, and became one of Her Majesty's Inspectors of Constabulary.

He was succeeded as Chief Constable by Mr Ronald Broome who came with a reputation as something of a horseman, which was demonstrated by his interest in and support for the Mounted Branch.

In 1983 the police horse *Somerset*, which had been a prizewinner in the Tent-pegging classes, was put down as a result of severe and untreatable lameness in both front feet. Like the recruit *Sulis*, *Somerset* had been a very quick horse, and when startled would jump in the air before the rider had a chance to compose himself, leaving the officer with his heart in his mouth and his stomach in his boots. *Ronald Broome*
In spite of this trait, and a mysterious dislike of white cars parked on the nearside, *Somerset* had been a competent police horse and the Section was sorry to see him go.

An even bigger equine name retired during October of the same year. Following an appearance in the Horse Personality Cavalcade at the Horse of the Year Show, when he was ridden by Chief Inspector Cheetham, police horse *Avon* bowed out and was given to the TV personality Noel Edmunds, who was willing to provide a home in retirement for him. *Avon* had been a Rolls Royce of a horse, with the ability to make even an average rider look good on him. He was also the last chestnut horse of the unit and his departure left us with a stable full of uniform-looking bays! *Avon* survived for a year in retirement with Noel Edmunds before dying of natural causes.

The Horse of the Year Show was of especial interest in 1983, because *Steele* would be attempting to win the title for an unprecedented third year. With PC Clarke's ability and *Steele*'s growing reputation, it was apparent that the Force had a powerful team which would be hard to beat - and so it proved. The championship was theirs again, and the Avon and Somerset monopoly was complete when *Kingsweston*, ridden by PC Dave Young, took second place. It was difficult to see how *Steele* could top this achievement, and few then could have foreseen that the horse was just in the early stages of a period of almost total domination at the Show.

The Christmas and January patrols of Broadmead were extended during the first few weeks of 1984 by regular patrols of the Bedminster Down area. The Division had been suffering from an unwelcome increase in house burglaries and walk-in thefts, and the Mounted Branch was requested to reinforce the local officers with saturation cover in the worst affected areas. The result was a dramatic improvement in the situation and after the initial swamping of the Down, regular excursions by individual mounted officers maintained the high-profile police presence. Other divisions of the Force were beginning to make similar use of the horses, and more and more mounted officers set off from

New line of stables at Bower Ashton

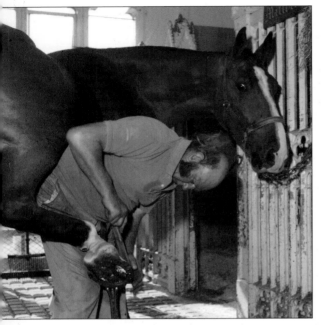

Farrier Monty Ball at work

Bower Ashton with a specific objective in view instead of a "general patrol" intention.

About this time, the deficiencies in the design of the main stable block at Bower Ashton were being recognised. Eight of the horses had to be housed in narrow stalls and for several hours of the day were forced to stare at the white walls. Not surprisingly, in their efforts to overcome the resultant boredom, some of them developed bad habits, such as pawing the ground or sucking at their mangers. It was decided to knock six of the stalls into three large boxes, and the accommodation deficiency was made up by building a further six boxes at the back of the premises next to the old railway line. These alterations were subsequently approved by the Police Authority, and the work was completed in 1984. All the horses could now be accommodated in spacious boxes, allowing them to move freely and observe the activities around them, which was a much better state of affairs. Two of the stalls were retained as a washing and clipping facility and for the use of the farrier who called each Wednesday to shoe three or four of the Section's thirteen horses - who had new shoes once a month on average. The farrier was Monty Ball from Winford, and his family had been shoeing the Bristol police horses for generations. The tradition is being maintained today by Monty's son, Andrew.

Two new horses joined the Section in 1984. The first was a large bay gelding, 17 hands high, who was later called *Yeovil*. He was bought to replace *Jubilee* who had died at Badminton the previous year. The horse was allocated to PC David Hurst. The second horse was *Kingswood* who was a more standard 16.2 hh, and he was allocated to PC Steve Nickerson. Around this time the Section was involved in a new operation which was to become more prevalent as the years progressed. The police amalgamation ten years previously brought the famed Beaufort Hunt within the Avon and Somerset area, and now the Hunt found itself the target for protest from a small but vociferous "animal rights" group which objected to the "barbaric" tradition of fox-hunting. The genuine anti-hunt protesters put their point across without stepping over the legal boundary but, as ever, the cause attracted a minority who sought every opportunity and means, lawful or otherwise, to disrupt the Hunt.

After some uncomfortable confrontations, the police at Chipping Sodbury requested the attendance of police horses at the Meet to prevent breaches of the peace and to deter hunt saboteurs from using illegal methods of protest. Later, when the protesters began to take to the fields to ambush the hounds and huntsmen, the police horses were obliged to actually follow the Hunt (at a discreet distance and at a more sober pace!) in order to be at hand if either a saboteur or huntsman over-zealously defended their philosophies. With animal liberation and protection groups proliferating over the ensuing years, this operation was to become a regular duty for the Bristol horses.

During the year, Chief Inspector Dick Cheetham was awarded the MBE for his work for the Constabulary, his chairmanship of the Avon Branch of the British Horse Society and his association with disabled riding charities. After his heart surgery in 1980 he appeared to make a full recovery and had maintained an active and enthusiastic leadership of the Section. In spite of the considerable physical effort required, he continued to lead the regular ceremonial escorts, and took much pride in the show successes of his unit.

Mr Cheetham had more cause to celebrate after the Horse of the Year Show 1984. In spite of every effort from the other Constabularies, *Steele* and Tony Clarke retained their grip on the trophy and won for the fourth year in a row. Their nearest challengers were once again stablemates *Kingsweston* and Dave Young, maintaining the monopoly

Chief Inspector Cheetham

of the previous year. The win was especially satisfying for the Chief Inspector as he was approaching the end of his career and the Show was to be the last one for him as officer-in-charge.

In March 1985 Richard Cheetham retired from the Constabulary, completing 38 years' service, 15 years of which had been as Horsemaster in the Bristol and then Avon and Somerset Forces. His intention in retirement was to continue with his stewarding and judging at local horse shows, and to take up the more relaxing pastime of bowling! Sadly however he had little time to enjoy himself, and his time as a police pensioner was cut cruelly short when he suffered another heart attack and died in December 1986.

Another Force Horsemaster was selected after Richard Cheetham's retirement, and the Horsemaster of the Cleveland Constabulary, Inspector Peter Griffiths, was chosen from the short list and promoted to Chief Inspector on taking up the post. Peter Griffiths was keen to involve the unit in more of the sporting classes for police horses at the shows. Consequently *Sedgemoor* and *Woodspring*, ridden by PC Gary White and PC Tim Liddeatt respectively, accompanied the Best Trained team of *Kingsweston* (PC Dave Young), *Steele* (PC Tony Clarke) and *Centaur* (PC Phil Jones) to several of the major shows that summer, with great success. *Kingsweston* and *Centaur* came 1st and 2nd at the South of England Show, and *Steele* won at the Staffordshire Horse Show. The Metropolitan Police Horse Show provided the Section with its first "Master-at-Arms" trophy, which was awarded to PC Tim Liddeatt and *Woodspring* for success in the Open Jumping, Team Jumping, Two Rings and Peg and Tent-pegging classes - all sporting events. The Horse of the Year Show 1985 also maintained the Avon and Somerset monopoly, except that on that occasion *Steele* and Tony Clarke had to be content with

Chief Inspector Peter Griffiths

2nd place behind *Kingsweston* and Dave Young, who became champions there for the first time. Chief Inspector Griffiths' first year in charge ended on a very satisfactory note and, in spite of the comparatively small size of the Branch, it was still apparent that the unit remained amongst the leaders nationally in police horse circles.

The round of ceremonial escorts continued unabated, and in the time-honoured dignified fashion - except one Legal Sunday morning, when we were to escort the Lord Mayor and HM Judges to a service at Bristol Cathedral. I was riding *Sulis*, who had been allocated to me after my previous mount *Jubilee* had died. *Sulis* had never been a comfortable horse to ride on formal occasions, and this time he decided that he had had enough of being on parade. He put in a couple of hefty bucks, which left me sprawling in an undignified heap on the ground, and then galloped off up the road. He must have felt a little lonely on his own, however, because he soon came back and I was able to remount and continue the escort with the only injury being to my pride! The incident provided a salutary reminder - if any was needed - that in spite of all their training, police horses remain animals and are subject to the fits and tempers of their kind. It is a tribute to the training of the horses and riders that this type of incident is fortunately rare!

The end of the football season 1985-86 also witnessed the last football to be played at Eastville Stadium, the home of Bristol Rovers. Following the disastrous fire which destroyed the South Stand in 1980 and in the face of demands for higher rent from the landlords, Rovers were forced to move across to Bath, and take up residence as tenants of Bath City FC at Twerton Park. The horses had been assisting at Eastville's matches for decades, and it seemed strange now to be heading in the opposite direction to police a ground which

WPC Davies and PC Goslin on duty at Eastville Stadium

was not ideal from a crowd control point of view. In later seasons, some hooligan confrontations took place in Twerton High Street, and mounted officers were often required to place themselves between opposing factions before forcing them apart and clearing the area. The narrow streets of this compact residential suburb of Bath were not ideal for the safe execution of some of the manoeuvres, and the officers had to be aware of the possibility of innocent bystanders being caught up in any mêlée which might occur.

PC Paul Bernard and WPC Sue Perry (nee Blanchard) both resigned from the Force in the early months of 1986 - Paul on a medical pension following an accident in 1984 and Sue to look after a baby daughter. The spring saw the Section involved with another display on the lawns in front of the Royal Crescent in Bath as part of the opening celebrations of the Bath Festival, and to mark the 150th anniversary of policing in the city. The display included a Cavalcade, Musical Quadrille and Tent-pegging exhibition, and was performed with great success in front of thousands of Festival-goers. The weather was kind to the Bath Festival event, but a few weeks later the Badminton Horse Trials were almost abandoned as a result of continuous heavy rain. The estate was turned into a quagmire and, although the police horses were able to continue patrolling, other means of transportation around the grounds proved impossible. There was talk of the event being cancelled, but fortunately the rain stopped in time and the competition went ahead. The later use of the Duke of Beaufort's washing box, where layers of thick mud were hosed off the police horses, was a facility appreciated by the animals and officers alike!

During the autumn of 1986 the Chief Constable of Dorset and Bournemouth requested the services of the Mounted Section once again, as part of his Force's effort to police the Conservative Party's annual conference which that year was to take place at the International Conference Centre in Bournemouth. Six horses and officers, including Chief Inspector Griffiths, spent the week as guests in a nearby military establishment and patrolled the town and sea front in the vicinity of the ICC. This was part of the height-ened security operation that had become necessary following the IRA bombing at the Conservative conference at Brighton in 1984.

The mounted patrols were welcomed by the townspeople, who

seemed to enjoy the novelty of police horses in their midst. Disruptions caused by demonstrations were minimal (although later a driver illegally attempting a forced entrance was prevented by a quick-thinking officer using a scaffolding pole to shatter the vehicle's windscreen) and the week ended with the horses supervising an orderly procession past the main entrance while the Prime Minister Margaret Thatcher was presenting her closing speech. The police operation was considered a success, and the Bristol mounted contingent returned home satisfied with the part they had played in it.

The Horse of the Year Show coincided with the Bournemouth operation in October, which meant that the Bower Ashton stables were almost deserted for the duration. The Bristol representatives were once again *Steele* ridden by PC Tony Clarke, and *Kingsweston*, the previous year's champion, ridden by PC David Young. *Steele* won the event for the fifth time in six years, and for good measure also won the Turn-out class. The older horse *Kingsweston* was second in the **Best Trained class** and in partnership with *Steele* also captured the Pairs trophy. Once again the prestigious show had provided a triumphant stage for the Avon and Somerset Mounted

Buffet reception at Bower Ashton following one of Steele's victories at the Horse of the Year Show. Mr Kenneth Steele (centre)

Branch, and the victory was celebrated in Bower Ashton with a short reception and buffet provided by the former Chief Constable Kenneth Steele - a party which was becoming an annual event!

After these two high-profile duties, the unit returned to the more mundane tasks of attending football matches at Ashton Gate and Twerton Park, and patrolling the Broadmead area in the run up to Christmas and beyond. Escorts for the Somerset Winter Carnivals also meant long, cold and noisy nights for the horses, and it was always with some relief that they returned to the warm, thick straw beds laid in their stables. The winter of '86-'87 was a particularly bad one, and during January Bower Ashton was snowed up to such an extent that the horses could not be allowed out. Although they are sure-footed in most conditions, it was just too dangerous to take them out amongst the traffic when vehicles were sliding all over the road. The stable yard had to be cleared of snow, and the horses were exercised by walking them around in a big circle - a very tedious business! Once or twice it was possible to use the large sloping field opposite the stables when several brisk gallops to the top, followed by more cautious descents, provided the necessary exercise.

Early in the New Year the partnership between *Steele* and PC Tony Clarke was ended when Tony was given the responsibility of training the new remount, later to be named *Wansdyke*. *Steele* was allocated to the experienced PC David Hurst, although it was agreed that Sgt Alan Jobbins would be *Steele's* rider during the showing season, including the forthcoming Horse of the Year Show when the horse would once again be defending his title as champion. Later in the year *Kingsweston* was retired after a distinguished career and thereby ended another remarkable chapter in the history of Bristol's police horses. *Kingsweston* had been an animal who needed to be ridden with some intelligence, as any heavy-handedness usually resulted in an opposite reaction to that intended by the rider!

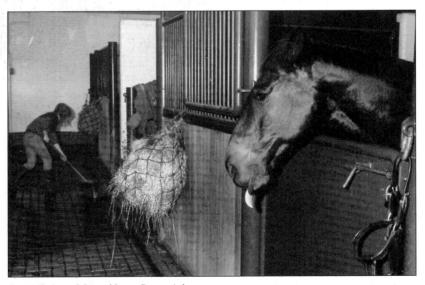

Internal view of the stables at Bower Ashton

During his first few months in charge, Chief Inspector Griffiths rearranged the pattern of shift work employed for the mounted officers, so that hours of duty corresponded more closely to periods of peak demand. Up until this time, a majority of officers would work on 'early turn' (starting at 6 am) in order to assist with the heavy stable work which was required at the start of every day. However, this meant that the officers completed their duty at 2pm. Normally this did not present a problem, but occasionally an operation would be requested which required working beyond 2pm, and this incurred considerable and expensive overtime.

The patterns were rearranged to provide for more cover during the periods 8am -4pm and 10 am-6pm. In addition the 'late' shift of 2pm-10pm was also utilised more during the summer months, in order to make the best use of available daylight hours when the horses were most effective. One officer was always employed on the 'late' turn as a stable man, to feed the animals and attend to their welfare until relieved by the 'night' turn officer. The late turn stable man was also required to act as guide for the many groups of interested people who two or three times a week toured the establishment. This was seen as an important part of our police-public relations effort, and most of the officers developed their own technique and patter to inform and amuse the visitors.

Trophy Cabinet in Ceremonial Room. Note the black tassel on the side wall of the showcase

I was responsible for one such group during the autumn of 1987. They were a party of young girls from a local riding school, and as usual I took them into the Ceremonial Room to show them the swords, lances, ceremonial equipment and trophy cabinet. I pointed out the black tassel which the Chief Inspector wears attached to his bridle for the Remembrance Sunday escort (on every other escort a white tassel was used) and asked the audience

PC Clarke with Steele at Bower Ashton

if they could guess which was the only occasion the black would be worn. I was faced with a row of blank faces for a few seconds, before one bright girl replied: "I know - he wears it on VD Day!" Not quite right, but I was able to repeat the story with some amusement to many subsequent visitors to the Ceremonial Room!

Towards the end of 1987 PC Tony Clarke retired from the Section to concentrate on running his farm at Shirenewton just across the Severn Bridge. During his mounted service he had been responsible for the training of numerous young police horses and had also ridden many to victory in various police horse classes up and down the country. He was a man who had a way with horses which was probably unique in police horse circles, and the Bristol unit benefited from his expertise and experience. In retirement he continued to break and train young horses for private owners, with great success.

Sgt Alan Jobbins rode *Steele* to a sixth victory in seven years at the 1987 Horse of the Year Show. He was by now assuming an invincible mantle, and was expected to win every time he entered the Show. However, it was as much a tribute to Alan's riding ability that he was able to repeat the success of previous years.

The following April witnessed the resignation from the Section of its first female member, WPC Diana Davies. After a shuddering fall during an Equitation Refresher Course she developed a problem in her back, and wisely decided to return to less rigorous duties while she could still walk! She was replaced by WPC Louise Downing, (later Smith) so the ratio of male/female officers remained the same at 4:1.

The same month six officers and horses made a return visit to Bournemouth, again at the request of the local Chief Constable. On this occasion the attendance was to assist in the policing of a football match at Dean Court, when the local team were playing Millwall FC. The London team's supporters had achieved the dubious distinction of being amongst the worst behaved supporters in the Football League, so the local police were taking no chances in their preparations for the game. As the game was "all-ticket", police intelligence indicated that several thousand ticketless supporters were going to make the journey to the south coast and attempt an entrance, which could have resulted in severe disorder. However at the last minute it was decided to relay the match via CCTV back to London, which kept the non-ticket holders away, and a 2-1 win for Millwall further reduced the potential for disorder among the visiting fans. The high-profile policing of the mounted officers completed the task and the event passed off peacefully, no doubt to the relief of the local inhabitants, who were beginning to get used to the presence of Bristol's horses!

WPC Davies on Brandon patrolling across Clifton Suspension Bridge

Public disorder was not confined to football crowds. Bristol's central division was sometimes the scene of drunken brawls on Friday and Saturday nights as youngsters celebrated the weekend. As an experiment it was decided to allow two mounted officers to patrol the streets around the busiest pubs and clubs until the small hours of the morning, in an effort to reduce tension and apprehend potential troublemakers. The officers were transported into the city centre by horsebox which was parked in the large Fire Station yard, and equipped with fluorescent jackets, leg spats and stirrup lights, off they ventured into the city centre. The riders were very wary of their patrol routes, because it was apparent that drivers were not necessarily on the lookout for horses on the streets at that time of night. The experiment continued for many months and, although the horses' presence was welcomed by both the divisional police and many of the citizens enjoying their night out, the results were somewhat inconclusive. There was some doubt that the risk to which the horses were subjected on the roads was worthwhile. It was decided that the regular excursions should cease but that the Section would be ready to respond to any further request from the Divisional Commander for assistance in specific operations in similar circumstances.

A Musical Ride display was prepared and practised for various events around the Force area for the summer of 1988. The first public display - a sort of "dry run" for the main events - took place at Stratton-on-the-Fosse in the Mendip Hills. It was not until the horsebox arrived on the site that the officers realised that there was going to be a problem. The arena in which the display was due to take place had been located immediately next to a children's bouncy castle - an inflatable monster with turrets waving in the breeze. It became apparent that none of the horses involved in the display were overjoyed to see it, but it was hoped that with *Centaur* leading the Ride the others would take courage from his example and ignore the thing. However, it was not to be! *Cumberland*, following *Centaur* towards the "monster", suddenly saw it and made a determined effort to escape. He shot across the arena with his rider vainly trying to stop him. *Kingswood*, immediately behind, must have thought that a new move had been inserted into the display and followed suit, in spite of rider PC Nick Barrett's efforts. In some embarrassment the four participants collected at the far end of the arena and continued the Ride, but the offending castle was noticeably given a very wide berth!

The later displays passed off without the same excitement and included two on Durdham Downs as part of a "Security Spectacular". The Princess Royal attended this event, and also performed a naming ceremony for the unit's new horse, *Taunton Deane*, ridden by PC Jeff Goslin. The horse had been donated to the Section by Min Mason, a long-time supporter who lived in Taunton, with the one proviso that it be named after her home town.

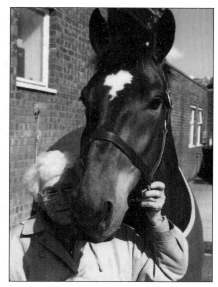

Min Mason with police horse Taunton Deane

The summer's showing schedule provided more success. At the South of England Show in Sussex, *Centaur* (PC Philip Jones) won the Best Trained trophy, with *Steele* (Sgt Alan Jobbins) coming in 5th. *Steele* later won the **Best Turned Out** prize, and the unit's involvement in the sporting classes continued with *Woodspring* (PC Tim Liddeatt) achieving 3rd place. The pattern was repeated at the Liverpool Police Horse Show. *Centaur* was champion again, with *Steele* 6th. When the Staffordshire Show came around, it seemed that *Centaur* was in the middle of an invincible run when he captured the **Best Trained** award yet again. The Kent Show spoiled the sequence, although *Centaur* was placed 2nd; but some consolation was gained when he and *Woodspring* won the Half-Section (Pairs) Tent-pegging competition. One of the Section's new horses, *Northavon*, also achieved some creditable results in various classes when ridden by PC Ian Hull, and it was hoped that the horse would develop into another winner in due course.

During the autumn the Section was involved for the first time with the "Scooter Rally" which was an annual event in the seaside town of Weston-super-Mare. This involved assisting local units throughout the day and into the night, helping to maintain public order on the streets of the town when enthusiasm combined with one drink too many resulted in an occasionally volatile situation. In later years the same operation was mounted to help police the "Enduro" competition, which involved racing motorcycles over a given course on the beach. The two events always attracted a large and enthusiastic following, and the police horses were invariably lent to the town for the duration where their presence on the streets helped to keep any disruption to a minimum.

1988 saw the establishment of a new record for the unit - yet another championship at the Horse of the Year Show. Again ridden by Sgt Alan Jobbins, *Steele* carried off the title for an amazing seventh time - making it eight years running that the title had come to Bristol. *Centaur* (PC Philip Jones), after a purple season, had to be content with 7th place. *Steele's* record at the Show, which was unprecedented after his third win, had now entered the unassailable category and his place in police horse folklore was assured.

Another new piece of equipment was added to the fabric of Bower Ashton during the latter half of the year. After the previous winter's problems, when horses had been manually exercised, a four-horse mechanical exerciser was established in one corner of the paddock. This enabled one officer to efficiently exercise four horses at once when required, and brought to an end the necessity of walking in hand during bad weather. It was a much-needed facility for the fitness and well being of the horses, and also became an aid to the efficiency of the Section. Events such as football matches and carnival processions did not of themselves provide sufficient exercise for the animals, especially if the horse was young or inexperienced. The animals could now be exercised before taking them into such situations, making their

"Go on, take another one of me...." George II feeling coy

presence safer and therefore more efficient. Planning permission for the Exerciser had of course been applied for in the usual way, but we noted that when it appeared in the Bristol Evening Post, a typographical error seemed to indicate that we had applied for permission to erect a four *house* walker! It came as no surprise that nobody objected to the scheme - curiosity about such an extraordinary piece of equipment must have been the predominant emotion! The exerciser was the first part of a larger scheme to establish an "all-weather surface" arena over part of the paddock to facilitate the training of officers, recruits and remounts. The surface was finally laid during 1990 and has since been regularly used to the benefit of the Section. However, as one officer complained when he returned dripping wet to the Tack Room, "It's all very well providing us with an all-weather surface - what we really need now are all-weather riders!"

Recruits to the Section continued to be trained by the two Sergeants, Gerry Haskey and Alan Jobbins, who alternately instructed internal Initial Equitation, (i.e. Learner's!) Courses. Before the advent of the riding surface, provided the weather was fine, training could take place in the paddock, but more usually the trainees and their mounts were transported to the indoor arena owned by the Avon Riding for the Disabled Association which was situated near Kingsweston Down. Once trained, the candidates had to return to their respective divisions and await a call to assist the department temporarily (usually during the summer months) before finally being transferred as and when vacancies occurred.

The police and football worlds were rocked in April 1989 by the dreadful tragedy at Hillsborough stadium in Sheffield, when nearly a hundred men, women and children were crushed to death at a Liverpool v. Nottingham Forest FA Cup game. The subsequent criticism levelled by the Taylor Report which investigated the tragedy shifted police emphasis at such events from crowd control to crowd safety, although of course the two elements were linked. The entire philosophy of policing football matches changed. Planning became more professional, and everybody involved in policing a game was required to attend intensive briefings to ensure a cohesive response to whatever problems arose at such events. Restrictive fences were torn down, and mounted officers with their elevated vision had to ensure that they surveyed crowded turnstile areas and terraces for signs of distress as well as for disorder. In general terms the duties of the mounted unit did not change as a result of the Report, but we were all made aware of how important it was to maintain a high level of supervision in order to help prevent such a tragedy occurring again.

During the early summer of 1989 Mr Ronald Broome CBE, QPM retired from the Avon and Somerset Constabulary, having served six years as its Chief Constable. He had always taken a keen interest in the business of the Mounted Section and was as pleased as anybody with the continuing Show successes. Before he retired he named the new remount *Plantagenet* - the name being derived from Middle English and Old French, meaning "sprig of broom". He continued to live in the area and was seen on more than one occasion supporting the Section's Internal Competition to which he had donated the **"Broome Trophy"** awarded to the horse and rider with the highest overall marks.

Mr Broome was succeeded by Mr David Shattock, who was returning to the Force he had joined in 1956. David Shattock had risen to the rank of Assistant Chief Constable by 1977, was later Deputy Chief Constable in the Wiltshire Constabulary and then Chief Constable of the Dyfed-Powys Constabulary, before returning to Avon and Somerset. He was well known as a horse lover from his previous time with the Force, and while in charge at Dyfed-Powys had also ridden a Cheltenham Gold Cup winner on exercise! More changes in the supervisory ranks at Bower Ashton occurred in May when the Dog Section Inspector, Brian Langley, retired and was succeeded by Inspector David McIver, a transferee from Dorset. Inspector McIver remained responsible for the Dog Section under the Horsemaster Peter Griffiths.

The summer of 1989 proved to be a very busy one for the Mounted Section. The Glastonbury Festival, also known as the Pilton Pop Festival, which had been held for twenty years at Worthy Farm, was now becoming so big that a considerable police operation was required to supervise it. Over 100,000 fans were crowded onto the site to hear top bands perform on the quirky "Pyramid" stage. Unfortunately drug abuse and petty crime was rife, so a police presence was desirable. Eight horses and officers, including Chief Inspector Griffiths and Sgt Alan Jobbins, remained billeted at the nearby Bath and West Showground and were transported to Worthy

Inspector David McIver

Farm each day to patrol designated areas of the camp and car parks. Some areas of the site were still, for want of a better word, anarchic, and the mounted patrols were limited to about two-thirds of the site. In the succeeding years inroads were made over the whole camp and there is now no such thing as a "no-go" area. In this first excursion, many of the law-abiding Festival-goers came up to us as we patrolled and said how pleased they were to see us out and about. They told us horror stories of the lawlessness that had prevailed in previous years, which had brought about the police response. The mounted unit remained on site all that week, finally returning to Bristol when the Festival was over late on a Sunday evening.

Soon after the Glastonbury event, the Chief Constable of the Wiltshire Constabulary at Stonehenge requested a mounted presence on Salisbury Plain. The occasion was the Summer Solstice and in previous years travellers had congregated there and damaged the stones. Severe disorder had broken out when the police had intervened, to the extent that for the 1989 Solstice an exclusion area had been declared around Stonehenge. The troublemakers had declared their intention of ignoring the exclusion zone, so the local police turned out in force, supported by their own helicopter and the Bristol horses. In the event no one actually broke through to

Stonehenge, although many tried and were apprehended as they approached the site. On horseback we were able to spot a few as they crossed the fields nearby, and using ground-to-air radio directed the helicopter with its "Night Sun" lamp towards them, when they were illuminated in its beam and arrested by police units on foot. The confrontation of the previous year was avoided and the stones protected. I was riding *Wansdyke* for this operation, and I was able to watch the sun rise on Midsummer Day from the middle of the stone circle - a real non-event, to be quite honest!

Sgt Gerry Haskey with two young visitors to the stables

The Community Free Festival was the next main operation for the mounted unit. This local Festival took place on the Ashton Court estate and, although not on the same scale as the Glastonbury Festival, still attracted thousands of people to listen to the music of local bands. Once again the main problems were theft and drug-related offences, but the high-profile presence of mounted officers assisted in maintaining good order and excursions through the dense woods nearby kept the drug offences to a minimum.

Further supervisory changes took place on the Section as the summer progressed. Sgt Gerry Haskey, who had transferred from the West Midlands on his promotion in 1975, completed 30 years' service and retired to take up a job as manager of the Avon Riding for the Disabled establishment. His good humour and general zest for the job had made him a popular supervisor, and the Section was sorry to see him go. A replacement was not immediately appointed, but PC Graham Hocking and I, as the only two officers with the group who had passed the qualifying examination, shared the role of Acting Sergeant.

In spite of the busy operational period, the Section was still able to send horses to the principle shows of the season. The early results were not so encouraging as in previous years, but *Woodspring* and Tim Liddeatt did manage to win the Tent-pegging class at the Staffordshire Show and also carry off the **Reserve Master-at-Arms** award. On the Display front, it was decided to abandon the Musical Ride and a new display was developed which was known as the Activity Ride. Whereas the Musical Ride set out to show off the

Part of the Activity Ride

basic training and paces of the animals, the Activity Ride was all about fitness and action as the team of four horses and riders were required to negotiate a series of small jumps in single file, as pairs, and in opposite cross-overs. The display also included a brief exhibition of tent-pegging, and taken as a whole presented a much more exciting show for audiences which were, after all, made up principally of *non-cognoscenti*. The Musical Ride had served us well over many years, but the time had come for a change.

The end of the summer activities did not signal a lessening of tempo. The early results of the local football teams were very good and led to a surge of interest and consequent bigger attendances at the matches. This was a particular concern at Twerton Park, especially in the light of the Hillsborough tragedy, and each match required the attendance of at least four, and sometimes six, horses. The season actually ended with both Bristol Rovers and Bristol City promoted to the Second Division, with Rovers going up as champions.

In addition to the local teams, the Section was also requested to send horses to help police matches at Swansea, Plymouth and Bournemouth. Vetch Field, Swansea was the scene of a European Cup match against the Greek team Panathanaikos, and in the first leg in Greece there was well-publicised trouble, resulting in some

PC David Young on Centaur with the Lord Mayor Kathleen Mountstephen and the Horse of the Year Show trophy 1989

Welsh fans being jailed. The return was expected to be as volatile, but careful segregation and close supervision by the mounted units over the departing fans prevented any repetition of the disorder.

During October Plymouth Argyle entertained First Division giants Arsenal in the Littlewood's Cup, and November saw the unit assisting at Bournemouth for a game against West Ham. Both these events meant long hours for the officers and horses, but with their help the operations passed off peacefully, and the host forces were happy to pay Avon and Somerset all the expenses incurred by the unit.

The last Horse of the Year Show of the 1980s saw the Section retaining the Police Horse of the Year award for the ninth year running - a staggering record. This time the champion was *Centaur*, ridden by PC David Young. *Centaur* had never achieved the adulation often accorded to *Steele*, but he was a grand horse, as honest as they come, and the success was well deserved. Alan Jobbins rode *Steele* into 4th place, which was itself a creditable performance; but it seemed that his success at the Show had finally come to an end.

The decade closed with the Section as busy as they ever had been in the field of operational work, both at home and around the region, and at the same time were maintaining a reputation for show-winning horses which was second to none.

CHAPTER NINE

CENTENARY DECADE

During the early months of the new decade feelings in the country ran high against the Government's proposals for a new tax to replace the old rating system. Some areas suffered from what became known as the "Poll Tax riots", and Bristol was no exception. A large demonstration took place on College Green in March, during which the Mounted Section was occupied in maintaining the peace and preventing the more excitable elements from storming the Council House. The horses were utilised on College Green and on the ramp leading to the Council House entrance and, although public disorder did ensue, the police were able to prevent any invasion of the building. Eventually the worst excesses of the demonstrators were restrained with the arrests of the ringleaders for public order offences. The situation remained ugly for some time, but was successfully contained with the help of the mounted units at the scene.

PC Liddeatt and Woodspring during the 'Poll Tax' demonstration 1990

Following on from Gerry Haskey's retirement the previous year, I was promoted to Sergeant in his place, and joined Alan Jobbins in the supervisory capacity, maintaining the mounted sergeant strength authorised in 1971. My place in the Tack Room was filled by PC Jon Green, an officer who owned his own horses and who thus already had considerable experience in the field of equitation.

Other changes in personnel occurred when early in 1990 two long-serving members left the Branch on transfer to other Divisions of the Force - PC John Burgess and PC David Gibbons. John Burgess had been a show winner when riding *Avon* at the Birmingham Show in 1968, and David Gibbons had ridden *Centaur* to success for three years running in the Force Internal Competition. They were replaced by WPC Rachel Vickery and PC Peter Wakely, who had the previous year safely negotiated their initial Equitation Course under the direction of Sgt Alan Jobbins.

The Activity Ride instituted with great success in the previous year was resurrected during the spring in preparation for appearances at major local events such as the Great Weston Air Day, Badminton Air Day and the International Caravan Club Rally at the Bath and West Showground - all of which attracted crowds numbering many thousands. The new action-based Ride was proving popular, but with the horses careering around the arenas at some speed it was important to ensure that the area in which the display was to take place was big enough to safely accommodate it. This reduced our appearances at the minor events, where fields were usually too small, but of course presented no problem to venues such as that at the Bath and West Showground.

Transportation was again becoming a problem. The Lambourn six-horsebox, purchased 11 years before, was now looking a bit worn out, after a decade of trundling horses and riders around the region! On two occasions the vehicle had broken down *en route* to operations, so Chief Inspector Peter Griffiths started looking around for a replacement. It came in the shape of a second-hand Volvo six-horsebox, which had been designed to transport shire horses. It was therefore considered robust enough to cope with police horses! After undergoing minor alterations and additions to comply with police requirements, and with a fresh coat of paint to transform it into the blue police livery, it began service in 1990.

During June, for the second year running, eight horses and riders of the Mounted Section were employed at Worthy Farm throughout the period of the Glastonbury Festival. After some logistical problems the previous year, it was decided to stable the horses in temporary accommodation set up in the police compound immediately adjacent to the Farm and to transport the officers each day from Bower Ashton. This gave us the opportunity to make the most of the available daylight hours in high-profile patrol work on the site, while one officer remained with the horses overnight to attend to their essential needs. Once again the Festival attracted a crowd conservatively estimated at over 100,000 strong, with drugs and theft offences being the main problem for the police. Gradually however, the whole event was being better organised, with perimeter fencing deterring some - but not all - of the gatecrashers. In later years a substantial double fence was erected, and one of the mounted unit's duties involved patrolling "no-man's-land" between the fences, and in the areas of the main gates, to prevent any breach of the peace as non-ticket holders attempted entry. The toilets provided for the Festival-goers remained primitive and inadequate, leaving many desperate campers to fend for themselves in the ditches and hedgerows. I always made a point of not patrolling my horse in such areas, remembering that I would later have to use a hoof-pick in his feet...!

The year saw the end of an arrangement with a local mushroom farm for the free collection of the manure produced by the stables. Country Kitchen Mushrooms had relieved us of the weight of the problem for many years, but now they were going over to the use of chicken manure. The days of free waste collection were obviously over, so following enquiries in the area the job was given to a commercial waste disposal company. This involved the use of a large rubbish skip and the demolition of the breeze-block-built manure pit that had served us for many years. However the new arrangements did not deter the local allotment owners from calling in to help remove some of the waste for their own use!

The first show of the season brought further success for *Centaur*, ridden by PC David Young. At the South of England Show the pair achieved 1st place in the Best Trained class. Alan Jobbins and *Steele* were 2nd, and they also gained 3rd prize in the Turn-out class. PC Tim Liddeatt riding *Woodspring* came 5th in the Tent-pegging class which always attracted a large entry of competitors.

The 1989-90 football season had finished with the two local League sides competing for the championship in a show-down at Twerton Park. A capacity crowd watched the game, which Rovers won 3-0. There was some disorder amongst the City fans during the game which prompted the City manager Joe Jordan to intervene as peacekeeper, and the use of foot officers and horses on the pitch-side. Although tension was high most fans enjoyed the occasion and in fact left the ground in an orderly fashion, even giving the mounted units standing by a round of applause!

The new football season soon showed that the problem of hooliganism was going to be difficult to eradicate, in spite of a greater awareness by the majority of the problems involved since the tragedy at Hillsborough. In September 1990 Bristol City played Newcastle United at Ashton Gate, and after the game a large group from Bristol attacked the Newcastle fans as they were being escorted along Ashton Road. We interposed the horses, and with the assistance of foot officers drove the hostile crowd up into North Street away from the Newcastle group. Coins and bottles were thrown at the police line, and a crowd of about 200 strong attempted to charge the line to return to Ashton Road. Under a hail of missiles the mounted officers were able to break up the crowd into smaller, more manageable groups. The officers had by this time drawn their staffs to protect themselves and their colleagues and, when one group attacked PC Graham Hocking and his mount, he struck two youths across the shoulders, causing them to run away and thereby dispersing the group. Gradually the incident died down, and those arrested were transported away to be charged.

Fortunately none of the mounted officers or horses were injured in the fracas, mainly thanks to the enveloping NATO helmet which was now the normal headwear for football matches and connected occurrences. However, the incident was just the beginning of a nightmare for PC Hocking and his family, as one of the youths whom he had struck had complained about the assault. Reports were submitted, PC Hocking's staff was examined, and a file was prepared with a view to prosecuting the officer. He was suspended from the job for a year until the matter came to Crown Court. As usual the Prosecution presented its case first, and those who were at the scene, including several independent witnesses, gave their evidence. At the conclusion of the prosecution evidence, before the Defence began to present its case, the Recorder referred to the jury to ask whether they needed to deliberate further. The answer was a unanimous 'No', and they returned a verdict of *Not Guilty*. The Recorder dismissed the case and remarked that "only in this country would such a prosecution have been pursued." Graham Hocking was immediately reinstated on the Branch, where he continued to work until his transfer to Trinity Road police station in 1997. The incident, though unusual in the lengths to which it went, demonstrated the real problems facing mounted officers as they set about the task of controlling unruly crowds.

The Horse of the Year Show at Wembley in 1990 brought to an end Avon and Somerset's dominance at the event. After nine years of non-stop success at the premier show, the run was at last broken when the title was awarded to a horse from the Merseyside Constabulary. On this occasion *Centaur* (Dave Young) was placed 3rd, and *Steele* (Alan Jobbins) was 5th. Although it was disappointing not to have won for a tenth year, the overriding emotion was one of pride, having set a record which was never likely to be challenged. *Steele* particularly had earned himself a niche in the history of the show, and the credit also reflected on his riders: Tony Clarke, who had laid such solid foundations in the animal's early training, and Alan Jobbins, who continued the good work against increasing competition from other Forces. *Steele* was, however, due to have a memorable swansong at the Show just four years later.

In January 1991 PC Gary White retired from the Force after 26 years' service, most of it with the Mounted Section. He had been *Justice's* rider when the horse had been killed on Clanage Road in 1973, and later had partnered *Cumberland*, *Avon* and *Sedgemoor*, the latter two horses with much success. WPC Julie Cannon replaced him on the Section. *Cumberland* retired a few months later, and the old horse was given to his former rider, WPC Diana Davies, who lived with her husband Huw in the tiny village of Chewton Mendip in Somerset. *Cumberland* settled comfortably into retirement in a nearby field equipped with stone-built stables until the whole family, including *Cumberland*, moved to Cornwall in 1997. During his period with the Section, *Cumberland* had established himself at the head of the pecking order amongst the horses, and even animals like *Sulis* (who was able to look after himself in most circumstances) always gave the older horse a wide berth when he was in the vicinity!

During January the Chief Constable David Shattock revived a little bit of history by riding on a full ceremonial escort of the Lord Mayor to a civic service at the city's Catholic Cathedral.

Apparently the last Chief Constable to have led a mounted ceremonial escort was Sir Charles Maby, who reputedly did so some time after the Second World War (although I could find no record of this during my research). However Sir Charles had certainly been equipped with all the uniform necessary for such an event, and David Shattock was actually able to wear Sir Charles' ceremonial tunic, which had survived in a reasonable state of repair. Riding on escort is a somewhat physically taxing affair, particularly for those for whom, like the Chief Constable, it is not a regular exercise; but he carried off the duty with some style. He later demonstrated a desire to improve his horsemanship in order to lead more escorts, but apart from leading the Remembrance Sunday escorts at a slow walk in the following years, an old injury to his knee prevented any further fulfillment of this ambition.

The districts of the Force were still regularly calling on the Section to assist in missing person searches, with the southern divisions and their wide open spaces making the most requests. During April the Bridgwater Division, which included Exmoor, initiated a "misper" search on the moor, as the missing person had last been seen in the vicinity of Selworthy Beacon. The four horses and riders involved commenced their search pattern from that landmark towards the village of Allerford. It is magnificent countryside, eminently suitable for riding. I was on *Wansdyke* for the search, and as the evening drew on, we found ourselves alone on top of a windy hill overlooking the Bristol Channel and retraced our steps through the dusk to the horsebox. I realised afresh how fortunate I was to be employed doing a job that was able to offer so much. The search itself proved negative (the missing person was later recovered on another patch of moorland) but the exhilaration of that evening ride in those superb surroundings was a memory which remains with me to the present day.

Regular visits were still being made to the primary schools in the Force area, with the children just as excited to be close to a police horse as they always had been a generation or two before. The days of the specialist Schools Liaison Team were drawing to a close, with the drive to make the most of existing Force manpower returning many to beat and Divisional duties. The requests for school attendance were now coming from the schools themselves, usually in order to further a project which the children were pursuing - "Working Animals" or "People Who Help Us".

Winners at the South of England Show 1991

The look on the children's faces as the horse appeared from around a corner in their playground and walked towards them was still, to my mind, worth the effort of getting to the school. In the Nineties the visit would usually have to be as part of a larger patrol in the area, as an hour's appearance for the children was no longer considered to be a practical use of police resources.

At the South of England Show at Ardingly in June, the Section maintained the good results achieved there during the previous year. *Steele* might have lost his crown at Wembley, but he was still a horse of some quality, and with Sgt Alan Jobbins as his rider he won the Best Trained class. *Centaur*, ridden by PC Ian Hull, came 3rd in the Best Trained and the Best Turned Out classes. At the same Show, *Woodspring,* ridden by PC Derek Tate, won the

Part of the Activity Ride

Individual Tent-pegging class, while *Plantagenet*, being ridden by *Woodspring*'s former rider PC Tim Liddeatt, achieved a very creditable 3rd in the same class - the horse's first attempt at a sporting event. The two shows following - the Metropolitan and Stafford Police Horse Shows - were not as successful, although WPC Rachel Vickery collected 2nd prize as Novice

Rider at Stafford, and PC Derek Tate and *Woodspring* missed winning the Open Jumping Class by knocking down the last fence of their second round! They had to settle for 3rd place. The Horse of the Year Show, later in the season, also disappointed with the main award going this time to the West Midlands Constabulary - although *Steele* did win the Best Turned Out class once again.

The Activity Ride was reintroduced during the summer, with displays taking place at Southampton (at the Hampshire Police Open Day), Bridgend (South Wales Police Open Day), Woodspring Equestrian Centre and at Hengrove Park for a local community function. The opening of the football season threw up the prospect of a double local derby, with City playing the Rovers in the first round of the League Cup, involving home and away ties. Fortunately the matches were trouble-free. The South Wales Police were also making more frequent requests for the attendance of mounted personnel at games involving Cardiff City and Swansea City, and a change of policy now required the host Force to be responsible for all the expenses incurred by the unit in their area - wages, cost of transportation, subsistence and the hire of the horses. The Cardiff City fans particularly had developed a bad reputation for rowdiness, and the use of horses in curbing the excesses at some of the more troublesome fixtures was now considered *de rigueur* by those dealing with the police response. The effectiveness of the Bristol horses' operations across the Severn Bridge was very soon to lead to the South Wales Police setting up their own mounted section, with the assistance of Sgt Alan Jobbins.

The Mounted Section was still also receiving regular requests to assist local personnel in the patrol of the various divisions of the Force, and the most recent applications were from the Southmead and Broadbury Road divisions. Southmead had their problems with the large estate off the Southmead Road, which always bubbled with some disorder or petty crime, and Broadbury Road suffered similar disturbances in the Knowle West estate. The mounted patrols were always a welcome addition to the attention paid by the local community constable, and their excursions into the troubled areas of the city were noted and appreciated by the majority of the local population. As Christmas approached the Bedminster shopping area received as much attention as Broadmead, with a view to reducing shoplifting and similar crimes which proliferated as the festive season approached.

*Lord Mayor's Coachman
Mr Ivor Morris*

In 1991 the Lord Mayor's stables at the rear of the Ashton Court mansion were closed, and the civic horses were removed to the Royal Mews. This ended a 200-year-old tradition, although the carriage continued to be maintained at Council expense. The ceremonial escorts were now maintained through the services of Michael Horler, a professional driver from Bath. The closure was a sadness for the Mounted Section who had maintained good relations with the Lord Mayor's stables and its coachman of thirty years, Mr Ivor Morris, who had recently retired.

New Year's Eve once again saw the Section dividing its resources throughout the Force area, and Central, Weston-super-Mare and Bath Divisions were each patrolled by mounted units as the midnight hour approached. The Abbey Churchyard was the scene for the revellers in Bath, and there was some concern over the security of the scaffolding shrouding the West Front of the Abbey. Although the Churchyard became packed with revellers just before midnight, the four horses and riders on duty there were able, by use of good humour and solid weight, to prevent anyone trying to scale the tempting scaffolding. One thing which the horses could not prevent, however, was their being kissed on the nose and face by the many horse-lovers in the crowd (usually girls!) and they were looking a bit wide-eyed by the time we got them back to the horsebox! Although the party passed off fairly peacefully in Bath, the two horses and riders employed in Weston were kept busy as disorder erupted in the town's High Street, and shop windows were smashed as the celebrations got out of hand. After assisting in quelling the disturbances, they arrived back at Bower Ashton much later than had been originally anticipated. The circumstances at Weston were noted in order that more attention could be paid for the following year's event.

On 1st April 1992, following a great deal of advanced planning and implementation, the Force underwent a major reorganisation with the intention of streamlining the service to ensure the best use of the limited resources available. One of the main objectives was to put more police officers back on the beat by releasing, in a process of civilianisation, police officers engaged in administrative duties such as those in Communication Centres and Custody Centres. Further developments of the reorganisation entailed a reduced management structure and the use of high-tech Force-wide computer equipment. The Force's 16 sub-Divisions were reduced to 11 "Districts", each commanded by a Superintendent. The Mounted Section did not escape the sweeping changes, and on the 1st April the post of Chief Inspector (Horsemaster) was abolished, and the practical and administrative leadership of the Section fell to the two mounted sergeants under the command of the officer head of the Dog Section, Inspector David McIver. Chief Inspector Griffiths was transferred to another police department and was located in an office in the recently opened Headquarters at Portishead; and so the post initiated with Percy Smith's promotion in 1955 was no more. Since the foundation of the Dog Section in the late '50s, the mounted supervisor had been titular head of the two sections, and now for the first time the hierarchy was reversed.

The Glastonbury Festival was revived once again that year, having had a year off in 1991. The weather was very hot and the conditions dusty as the eight horses and riders on duty patrolled the site.

PC Jeff Goslin on Sedgemoor and PC Nick Barrett on Kingswood patrolling at the Glastonbury Festival

An additional problem was the setting up nearby of several illegal "raves", which had to be dismantled by the authorities in the face of opposition from the persons involved. The mounted units assisted in maintaining order at these events, but it was while *en route* to such a job that *Centaur*, ridden by PC Ian Hull, stumbled and fell onto his knees, leaving nasty wounds which necessitated his return to Bristol, and eventually ended his career. He was replaced at Glastonbury by the young horse *Brunel* who acquitted himself well, in spite of some bemusement at all the goings-on!

On the final day of the Festival, four horses were withdrawn early from the site in order to go to the Royal Crescent in Bath where the world-renowned tenor, Jose Carreras, was giving a recital. The show was attracting thousands into the Royal Victoria Park, but of more concern was the threat from a group calling itself "Class War", whose intention was to disrupt the concert. However, the group's adherents were never allowed to get anywhere near the event, which passed off peacefully. The mounted units patrolled the perimeter of the temporary auditorium set up for the concert and were left to muse on the cultural shock they had endured in exchanging the rock bands at Glastonbury for the mellifluous tones of Carreras in the Royal Crescent!

Police horse *Brandon*, who had joined the Section in 1974, was retired that summer to a family in Lower Claverham, where the facilities included a well-appointed stable and a five acre meadow for the horse's use. If any horse ever deserved a good home, it was *Brandon*. He had been a real favourite because of his genial disposition and gentle nature, and was a horse you could trust in any circumstances. *Brandon* was frequently chosen by the Horsemaster to carry him on ceremonial duties, and never once did the horse give any cause for concern whilst on parade. In his last few years *Brandon* developed a little habit of putting his head over the stable door and blowing raspberries at any passers-by, so whenever I showed visitors around the place I always approached his box hoping he was going to perform for them. He rarely let me down!

The summer operations continued apace, with mounted involvement at the Royal Bath and West Show, on Inglestone Common (which had been the scene of a near-riot amongst the traveller fraternity in previous years), at Brean and Berrow to patrol the beach and dunes for the prevention of indecency offences, and up into the Quantock Hills, where attention was paid to the car parks to help reduce thefts of and from unattended cars. As always, Weston-super-Mare was accorded a high priority, with the summer influx of visitors creating a heavy workload for the local police.

The Activity Ride displays were fitted in around the police operations, and during the summer the display was presented at the Royal Victoria Park in Bath (as part of the opening celebrations of the International Music Festival), at Thornbury Motorama, at the Garden Festival at Ebbw Vale and the Community '92 Family Festival run by the Force in Ashton Court. All the displays were well attended by the public, especially the Bath event. The display team consisted of *Woodspring* (PC Derek Tate), *Plantagenet* (WPC

PC Green's right boot and PC Wakely's right ear in close proximity!

Louise Smith), *Wansdyke* (PC Jon Green), and *Kingswood* (PC Nick Barrett). The backdrop for the display was the Royal Crescent, and the event went very well, except that *Plantagenet* demolished his first jump (a tea-table with two ground-crew taking tea), which rather startled *Wansdyke* following on behind. He jumped off to the side, which resulted in Jon Green giving one of the ground crew an unscheduled kick in the ear! Needless to say, the local press photographer was at hand to record that very moment, and even though the rest of the display went like clock-work, that was the image portrayed in the newspaper the next day!

The showing season got off to a good start when *Centaur* (PC Ian Hull) won the Best Trained class at the South of England Show. This was *Centaur*'s last appearance in the show arena in which he had performed so creditably over the years, and the accident at the Glastonbury Festival ended another notable equine career. The only entry for the Horse of the Year Show this year was *Steele* (ridden by WPC Rachel Vickery who had recently been allocated the horse) due to the event coinciding with a high priority football match at Ashton Gate. The pair performed commendably in achieving 2nd place.

New Year's Eve was again a busy night for the Section and, in the light of the previous year's problems, four horses and riders were despatched to assist the district police at Weston-super-Mare. The High Street was filled with celebrating people, but on this occa-sion the festivities remained good-natured and the mounted units were able to patrol without involvement in the type of disorder experienced by their colleagues in the previous year.

In March 1993 PC David Hurst retired from the Section. His experience of the job had been put to good use in the years of his service, when he was frequently required to ride and train the younger inexperienced horses. He was replaced by the Section's fourth female member, WPC Shirley Yeatman.

The highlight of the showing season that year was the trip to the Metropolitan Police Horse Show at Imber Court, and for once it was the sporting classes in which the Avon and Somerset horses and riders excelled. In the Provincial Tent-pegging class *Taunton Deane* (PC Philip Jones) gained 1st prize. *Woodspring* (PC Derek Tate) was 3rd and *Kingswood* (PC Nick Barrett) was 6th. In the Championship of the same class, which was run off against the winners of the Metropolitan class, *Taunton Deane* was awarded 1st prize and the championship. *Woodspring* came 2nd. To complete the tent-pegging whitewash, the Team Tent-pegging trophy was won by the Avon and Somerset team, with 2nd and 3rd prizes going

L to R: PC Philip Jones; PC Derek Tate; PC Nick Barrett after Imber Court 1993

to the South Yorkshire and Lancashire forces respectively. In the Sword, Lance and Revolver preliminary class *Woodspring* won 1st place and was eventually placed 2nd in the championship. As a result of the prize-winning combination in the tent-pegging classes, PC Philip Jones was awarded the **Metropolitan Police Master-at-Arms** trophy - the first time the unit had won it since PC Tim Liddeatt had achieved the accolade eight years earlier. 185 competitors from twelve constabularies and four military detachments took part in the Show, and the results therefore represented a considerable achievement by the Avon and Somerset team, coming as they did from one of the smallest establishments in the country.

The 1993 football season started reasonably quietly for the unit, but all that changed in September, when South Wales Constabulary requested the assistance of the Branch at a European Cup Winners Cup match as Cardiff City took on the Belgian team, Standard Liege. There had been considerable disorder in Liege at the first game, and it was feared that similar scenes would be repeated in Cardiff. All went well until after the game, when a large group of Cardiff fans attempted to rush the Liege fans' exits. The mounted units managed to divert them and shepherd them away, but the hard-core hooligans continued with the disorder. For an hour, as the horses pushed them further from the ground, they were bombarded with stones, beer glasses, bottles and bollards. Three of the officers - PC Jeff Goslin, PC Jon Green and

PC Nick Barrett - received minor injuries from the missiles as the melee continued, until finally the crowd was dispersed and the Belgian fans moved away without further mishap. It was plain that without the intervention of the mounted units serious disorder would have ensued, and their use in the situation was fully vindicated. Mr David Shattock later received a letter from the Assistant Chief Constable of the South Wales Police expressing the gratitude of his Force for the assistance the Mounted Branch had been able to provide.

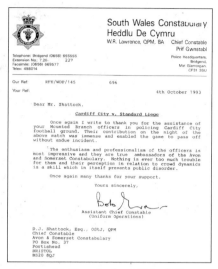

Letter received from the South Wales Police

Once again the Horse of the Year Show came and went without a winning entry from the Bristol stable. The Somerset Carnivals continued to keep the unit busy throughout the autumn, culminating in a final procession through the streets of Bristol. However the run up to Christmas and the New Year was to bring anything but good cheer to the Section. Following on from the reorganisation of 1992, and as part of the continuing review of the Force and all its various departments, it appeared that a move was afoot either to drastically reduce or disband the Mounted Section. The arguments which had been used against the Branch in 1920, 1930 and to a lesser extent in 1969 rose to the surface again. The financial restraints on the whole Force made a severe examination of its practices a necessity, and voices were raised in support of the disbandment of the "anachronistic" mounted unit. An article appeared in the local press to report that the "award-winning Mounted Section" might be sacrificed by "the cash-strapped Force". The arguments swayed back and forth amongst the force hierarchy and in the Police Authority (the old Watch Committee) until a meeting of the Authority (making a decision which was awaited with some trepidation!) confirmed that the unit would be retained but that it would have to undergo a reduction in staff and horses. The numbers of staff were to be reduced from sixteen officers to twelve, and the horses reduced from thirteen to ten.

Four mounted officers had to leave the unit, and two departed almost immediately. WPC Rachel Vickery transferred to the Yeovil District to pursue her ambition of promotion (she had recently qualified), and PC Tim Liddeatt retired on a medical pension when an old knee injury failed to respond to treatment. Both officers had made an impact on the Section, and Tim Liddeatt especially had made his mark in the enthusiastic and reliable pursuit of a job he loved. It was rather ironic, in the days of imminent reduction, that the mounted unit was asked to provide a total of fifteen horses at various venues around the Force to assist with the policing of the New Year's Eve celebrations! The Section concentrated on the places that had given cause for concern in the past. Ten horses were also turned out for a Bristol City v. Liverpool Cup match in the New Year. Minor disturbances occurred both before and after the game, to which police commanders were happy to send mounted units as part of their response.

The spring of 1994 brought me a job that has lodged in my memory. It was an operation which required that *Steele* and I remain in the background to keep an informal eye on proceedings while the former President of the Soviet Union, Mikhail Gorbachev, visited the Bristol-based charity CLIC (Cancer and Leukaemia in Childhood) which was based in Fremantle Square. Gorbachev had recently accepted an invitation to become International President of the charity, and a large crowd had gathered to see him enter and leave the building. They gave him a rousing reception, indicative of the warmth of feeling generally felt towards him. As I watched, I couldn't help feeling how strange it was to see this man, who at the height of his power had taken the salute of the Army in Red Square, Moscow, now accepting the plaudits of Bristolians in Fremantle Square. I wondered what odds I would have got only a few years before, on such an event ever happening?

Two more officers volunteered to leave the Section during the next few months and thereby obviated the necessity for a mandatory transfer imposed from outside the unit. PC Jeff Goslin who had joined the Mounted in 1980 now transferred to the Criminal Justice Unit at Broadbury Road police station to see out the last few months of his service before retirement. Later, WPC Julie Anthony (previously Cannon) returned to work with a Support Unit at Avon Street after three years "in the saddle".

The three horses selected for retirement were *Centaur*, *Sulis* and *Redcliffe*. *Centaur* was retired to his old home at Burnham-on-Sea, and in fact went back into a paddock with his mother! (One can imagine her saying, as *Centaur* entered through the gate and trotted over to her -"And where d'you think you've been all this time?"). He had never fully recovered from the accident at Glastonbury Festival, in spite of constant nursing from the civilian groom Brenda Hapgood, and was therefore an obvious choice.

Sulis was also approaching the end of his service, and a reluctance on his part to travel in the horseboxes meant that his operational usefulness was already curtailed. Bearing in mind his propensity for biting and kicking, we were obliged to find him a home with experts, and this turned out to be at the Home of Rest for Horses in Whitchurch. He had been a marvellous practical police horse in his time (he was my allocated horse for five years) and I was sorry to see him go, but when I visited him several months later, he was looking quite relaxed and content in his new surroundings. I noted however the warning sign on the door of his box - it was obvious that retirement was not going to change this character! The third horse, *Redcliffe*, was a big youngster who, it was decided, would do better in a career outside the police service, and he was sent to join the Household Cavalry who value his stamp of animal.

A further consequence of the examination of the practices of the Mounted Branch resulted in the adoption of a new policy (or restatement of an old one?) that the horses would not compete in any more Shows. In addition it was decided that the Branch would no longer perform Activity Rides or Musical Rides. The objective of these decisions was to save police time in the preparation and training for these events and to demonstrate a total commitment to the operational work of the group. In fact the show veto was relaxed a little later when it was agreed that we should send a representative to the Horse of the Year Show scheduled for October. However for all we knew this would be the last such event in which the Branch would ever participate and would thus bring to an end a proud page in its history.

The month of October also brought a request from the Chief

The last Activity Ride. L to R:Sgt. Foulkes, WPC Louise Smith on Plantagenet, PC Jon Green on Wansdyke, PC Nick Barrett on Kingswood, PC Philip Jones on Taunton Deane. Note Volvo horsebox in background.

Constable of the Dorset and Bournemouth Constabulary to provide five horses to assist with the policing of the Conservative Party Conference. Like the conference of 1986, this was to take place in the International Conference Centre in Bournemouth, and there were fears that recent objections to the proposed Criminal Justice Bill would erupt in disorder in the town. The local police also enlisted the support of five police horses of the City of London Police, which brought the strength of the mounted contingent to ten. Like the operation in 1986, the officers and horses were billeted in a nearby Marine camp and patrolled in the town and around the Conference Centre each day. The week passed off relatively quietly and, although a large number of people objecting to the Criminal Justice Bill joined a march from a local park to a demonstration outside the Centre, the two groups of horses from Bristol and London presented a solid front for the procession and were able to supervise the event without undue disorder.

So to the Horse of the Year Show, 1994. The only representative from Avon and Somerset was *Steele*, ridden by Sgt Alan Jobbins. We were all hoping that the old champion would turn it on for just one more time to enable his showing career, and that of the Section, to be appropriately crowned with another title. In view of *Steele's* recently declining fortunes we knew it was a tall order, and the chances were further reduced when their opportunities for training were curtailed by a rush of operational duties. As it turned out, the competition was as fierce as ever, with some good horses from other Constabularies making an excellent impression. *Steele* however was not a multiple champion for nothing and, bringing to bear his experience in the event coupled with Alan's expertise, he won the

Sgt Alan Jobbins and Steele negotiate the 'nuisances' at the Horse of the Year Show 1994

dressage phase and was by far the steadiest through the Street Nuisance test. He won the trophy for an amazing eighth time, setting a new record which was never going to be bettered. The horse was retired from competition after the event, so it was an emotional time for all concerned. We thought then that the Showing Book had been closed for good, and as it transpired the class for police horses was to remain in existence for two more years. As pressures grew for national mounted units to be totally operationally orientated, support for the police horse class diminished to the extent that 1996 became its final flourish. The proud record of the Bristol, and then Avon and Somerset, police horses was going to remain unchallenged.

In January 1995 PC David Young, who had joined the Section during the summer of 1975, retired on a medical pension. He had ridden both *Kingsweston* and *Centaur* to many show successes, including the two horses' only victories at Wembley, and towards the end of his career he gained accreditation as a rider trainer. An unsuccessful operation to an old shoulder injury put paid to any ambitions he may have had in that direction and he retired to become an inspector for the horse welfare group, the Horses and Ponies Protection Association. He was replaced by WPC Kerry Nichols.

The training qualification gained by PC Young was part of a concentrated effort, devised by the National Mounted Conference with Home Office prompting, to standardise training procedures throughout the mounted police world. As a long-time member of the Conference, Sgt Alan Jobbins was seconded to help develop the new scheme; and he was certainly well placed to do so with his qualifications and experience in both the police and civilian horse-riding worlds. Training was after all a strenuous physical activity which entailed a high risk of accident or injury, and the intention was to reduce the risk of any possible future litigation being launched on the grounds that the trainers were not properly qualified. Two other officers, PC Nick Barrett and PC Jon Green, also later gained the training accreditation. Other tests of efficiency were applied to the regular members of mounted branches in order to bring the standards to as high a level as possible. Several members of the Bristol group passed these tests within a few months of their instigation.

When the new phase of Police Headquarters at Portishead was officially opened by Queen Elizabeth in June, the Mounted Branch provided a guard of honour as she entered and left the building. Sgt Jobbins and *Steele* were presented to her at the event, and she spent several minutes talking to Alan and admiring the horse. *Steele* in fact tried to eat the Queen's posy, and was only finally dissuaded when she walked away! Being a horse lover herself, the Queen was not in the least put out.

The Glastonbury Festival monopolised the Section's attention at the end of June, and eight horses were again stabled in temporary accommodation in the police compound at Worthy Farm. The two unused horses were turned out to grass, and the mounted establish-ment at Bower Ashton virtually shut down for seven days as the operation proceeded. The horses and riders now patrolled over every inch of the enormous site, including the car parks and between the perimeter fences. The Festival had grown to such pro-portions that the police operation was required to commence sev-eral days before the event itself. It would continue for two days afterwards to assist in the evacuation of the site.

So the summer progressed without the interposition of shows or displays. The Community Free Festival at Ashton Court attracted many thousands of Bristolians who enjoyed the varied programme provided by the organisers, and the Mounted Branch patrolled the site which was a convenient few hundred metres from the base at Bower Ashton. The football season recommenced in August and

Mounted units assist in restoring order at Ashton Gate

was destined to be the last full season played by Bristol Rovers as tenants of Bath City FC at Twerton Park. The regular haul over to the stadium had been a feature of mounted life for ten years, and no one was sorry that Rovers' attempts to relocate back in Bristol now seemed to be bearing fruit when an agreement with Bristol Rugby Club to use the Memorial Ground meant that they could commence the '96-'97 season back near the hotbed of their support. A short trip up the Gloucester Road was infinitely preferable to the often tortuous drive to Bath!

In January 1996, as a consequence of City's relegation in the previous season, the first League derby for three years took place between City and Rovers at Ashton Gate. The official attendance at the game was put at 20,007 people. There was considerable disgruntlement before the kick-off, when thousands of ticket-holders were turned away when the stadium became full, the arrangements for admittance having broken down by an administrative blunder. The anger expressed as a result of the blunder was totally understandable, but the reaction of a section of City's fans in the Dolman Stand when Rovers won the game 2-0 was anything but justified. Hundreds of them swarmed down the steps of the Stand in an attempt to get at the Rovers fans situated at the Covered End of the

Steele, Police Horse of the Year 1981/82/83/84/86/87/88/94

ground, and the mounted officers and foot police were obliged to race around the edge of the pitch to prevent the invasion. A line of horses provided a barrier that stopped the crowd in its tracks, but their frustration was vented on the advertising boards lining the pitch, which they proceeded to destroy and throw around. Gradually the mob was pushed back and the game continued. However the atmosphere remained threatening and at the final whistle the horses interposed themselves again between the two sets of fans. Fortunately the ground was evacuated without similar disorder. The whole incident showed the potential for disaster, especially in the light of Hillsborough, when such a large crowd assembled in a confined space with an unruly element intent on trouble. The mounted officers later patrolled the environs of the ground until the crowd had dispersed, and was yet another demonstration, if any was needed, of their effectiveness in that type of situation.

In March 1996 *Steele* retired from the Section and was sent to live on an estate in beautiful surroundings just outside Abergavenny. Not much more needs to be said about him after a career of such unpar-

*PC Darryl Snow on Matthew, Sgt Alan Jobbins on Steele, with
CC David Shattock and Mr Kenneth Steele*

alleled excellence, and his record at the Horse of the Year Show will
stand as a memorial to a remarkable horse. He was replaced on the
Section by a youngster which was named *Matthew* in a ceremony on
the harbourside adjacent to the replica of John Cabot's famous ship
of the same name. The horse was to be trained by PC Darryl Snow
who had joined the group in 1985 and had for some years been
demonstrating an ability in the field of remount training.

My own retirement came in the following month. I had spent
21 years with the best job in the Force, as I termed it, and I left
to pursue other interests. On retirement I was privileged to
receive from the Lord Mayor Mrs Joan McLaren, the Lord
Mayor's Medal which was awarded for services to the ceremonial escort. The authorised strength of the Section was revised
after my departure, and Alan Jobbins was left as the only
Sergeant - a return to the position Percy Smith had occupied
until after the Second World War.

Mounted officers on duty at Ashton Gate. Compare equipment with the photos on page 113

As a consequence of the staff reduction in the previous year, it became necessary to review the working practices of the group, in an effort to make the most of the resources now available. An officer had been employed on a night shift at Bower Ashton since 1971 with a view to maintaining the security of the premises and ensuring the welfare of the horses. This meant of course that the officer was thereby removed from the operational strength of the group for nearly two weeks, taking into account the rest days before and after the seven-night shift.

A more efficient use of the time was now required in the light of the staff reduction, and it was decided to abolish the stable night duty and return the officer to more valuable operational duties during the day. The late shift officer was required to ensure that the horses were settled in for the night before setting all the alarms and locking the premises at the completion of his duty. Night security then became a matter of electrical surveillance; but in fact the security of the premises was enhanced by the installation of new alarms in addition to the overnight use of the premises by the dog handlers. Often, the dog section supervisor would also remain on station all night, completing his administrative tasks.

Towards the end of the summer 1996 *Wansdyke* was retired to pasture in the Thornbury area and was replaced by a remount which was later named *Somerset*. *Wansdyke* was a big, good-looking Cleveland Bay who had been my allocated horse for some years and had proved to be a competent police horse, although inclined to nervousness. However, he was able to warn his rider of impending problems by twisting his nose up and to the side, as if he was an elephant looking for buns! His riders very soon learnt to watch for this tell-tale sign!

The horses were again utilised on the south coast in October, when they patrolled Bournemouth during the Conservative Party Conference. The event passed off peacefully, but the new football season brought with it more evidence that the misbehaviour that had blighted the game for nearly thirty years had not been entirely eradicated. Once again the flashpoint occurred after a derby game in December between Bristol City and Bristol Rovers at Ashton Gate. A late equalizer for the visiting team brought some Rovers supporters onto the pitch (itself a specific offence under new legislation) and the sight was enough to encourage some hot-headed City fans to do likewise. When the referee blew for full-time a few

A rare moment of relaxation during the operation in Bournemouth 1996

moments later, it heralded a mass invasion of the pitch from the Dolman Stand and some players, unable to reach the safety of the Atyeo Stand, were forced to seek refuge in the old stand. The police horses were deployed along the front of the Dolman Stand to prevent further trespass and to assist in clearing the pitch. Sadly for football in the region, the game had been televised live on a Sky Sports channel, sending the worst possible images around the nation. There was at least the benefit of camera identification for the main offenders who later faced heavy penalties and were banned for life from the football ground.

The latter end of 1996 and the early months of 1997 saw the retirement of two of the Section's longest serving members, both of whom had, in their own way, made a lasting impact on the group. PC Philip Jones joined the Mounted Section in 1969 just before the expiration of his two year probationary period and had thus spent almost his entire career "in the saddle". His interest in horses and riding stemmed from an involvement, at an early age, with the Banwen Pony Club in his home area of South Wales, and in fact he had competed for his local club at events in the Horse of the Year Show. The competitive nature of his riding was further demonstrated throughout his career when he won many police horse classes around the country on a number of different horses from the Bristol stable. As his experience grew he was often selected to ride, manage and educate the more difficult mounts of the Section. On his retirement he was presented with a painting depicting the horses allocated to him in his 28 years on the Branch, and apart from a couple of notable exceptions the picture looked like a veritable "rogues gallery" of animals to those of us who had had the pleasure of their acquaintance! It said much for Philip's attitude and persistence that he invariably made a success of his partnerships.

The other retirement was that of Sgt Alan Jobbins. He had joined the Mounted Section in 1971, completing 26 years with the group. His natural ability as a rider, aided by an intelligent and practical interest in all things equine, was put to good use by the Section, and he became a successful horse and rider trainer whose reputation had spread nation-wide by the time of his retirement. His involvement in the deliberations of the National Mounted Conference, and his assistance in the setting up of the South Wales Mounted Branch, were just two examples of the use to which his talents were put. In 1995 he had been seconded by the Home Office to play a leading role with HM Inspectorate of Constabulary in the evolution of the new *National Mounted Branch Training Development Plan*, which was re-shaping the national training philosophy for mounted units. He had won many trophies for the Branch during his career, the highlight of which was, he would probably agree, the winning of the Police Horse of the Year title on *Steele* in 1994. He had trained many of the recent and current members of the Section, all of whom could pay tribute to his abilities in this field and the benefits they had acquired as a result. He was replaced on his retirement by Sgt Andrew Bishop, who transferred from the Sussex Constabulary and who earlier in his career had had several years experience with the Mounted Branch of the Metropolitan Police.

The following summer saw the Mounted Section utilised in quelling a violent demonstration by "Anti-Road Protesters" in the Bond Street and St James Barton areas of the city. Bond Street was blocked by a large group of demonstrators, many of whom were drunk. Missiles were thrown and shop windows were broken, putting the police and nearby shoppers, including children, in danger. Later PC Darryl Snow, who had been riding *Taunton Deane* at the demonstration, discovered a hypodermic syringe sticking in his saddle near his leg, which had apparently been thrown at him during the fracas. The consequences had the needle struck him or the horse could

PC Jon Green on Yeovil at the Anti-Road demonstration, St James Barton

have been horrific, but fortunately the thick leather provided sufficient protection and no damage was done.

The Mounted Section's involvement in police operations continued as the summer progressed, with the unit once again sending eight horses and riders to help supervise the enormous crowds which flocked to the site on Worthy Farm for the Glastonbury Festival, reinstated after two years off. Unfortunately the weather was very wet, and the campsite soon turned into a nightmarish quagmire, making progress around the various attractions at best uncomfortable, and at worst very difficult. The police horses continued patrolling through the mud where access with motor vehicles was proving impossible, and maintained the high-profile presence which had helped drag the event from the edge of unfettered criminality just a few years before. The majority of this year's Festival-goers had to make the best of the weather, and often frolicked in mud-baths and generally behaved in the Bohemian style which many had adopted for the duration! There was more than the usual relief for the horses and riders, however, when the operation was concluded and they were able to return to the welcoming dry warmth of the stables at Bower Ashton!

More crowd disorder was encountered during the early stages of the ensuing football season of 1997-1998. In November the fixture between Bristol City and Millwall at Ashton Gate ended with large groups of opposing fans fighting on the concourse around the perimeter of the stadium, and the intervention of mounted officers and dog handlers was required to restore order. It was apparent that the police still could not afford to drop their guard at such events.

Sedgemoor, another good and faithful servant of the Branch over many years, was humanely destroyed during the autumn of 1997, when a continuing painful lameness was making life miserable for the old horse. He had been a friendly and sprightly animal in his prime, often representing the Force in partnership with PC Gary White, in the latter stages of police show-jumping events. He had also been a confident and competent operational police horse, although sometimes he did exhibit a predisposition to face whatever nuisances and noises were about. This meant that his rider often found himself looking straight at a brass band which they were supposed to be leading! As long as *Sedgemoor* could see what was going on, he remained happy!

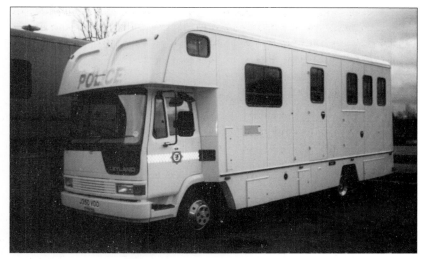

The new Leyland horsebox, 1998

The Christmas and New Year period brought with it the usual rush of Force-wide police operations for the Mounted Section, and in fact the unit was involved in over 60 such duties during this time. It included a very long night for two officers and horses who attended a New Year "rave" at the Bath and West Showground, followed by a visit to Bath to help supervise the celebrations there. Their presence assisted in maintaining public order at both events.

Early in 1998 the Branch disposed of the old Dodge horsebox which had performed sterling service since 1982 but was now worn out. As replacements they took possession of two new Leyland vehicles capable of transporting 4 and 2 horses, and both of which provided good accommodation areas. Appropriate transport could now be used for the various operations, with the 2-horsebox particularly valuable in moving the horses and riders around the region in a more economical way.

* * * * *

And so the Mounted Section founded by the Bristol Constabulary, and maintained by its successor the Avon and Somerset Constabulary, approaches its centenary year. Few institutions born at the beginning of the century survive to witness the new millennium, and many of those which do are barely recognisable in comparison with their counterparts of 100 years ago. The Mounted Branch has survived largely intact, and looking back down the century can take pride in the role it has played in helping to maintain peace and good order in this part of the kingdom throughout a turbulent and fast-changing era. Now may be the appropriate time for the police horse, in partnership with his human colleagues, to take a well-deserved bow!

PC Wakely and Kingswood hand out a little friendly advice!

Chapter Ten

Into the New Millennium

By way of a short epilogue, I have set myself the task of attempting to answer the question which may be on the reader's mind - is there still a future for the Mounted Section, when the modern police service can call on the most extraordinary achievements of science and engineering to assist in the eternal fight against crime? The success of the police helicopter and the appliance of DNA testing are just two of the advances which spring to mind, and it may be difficult to assimilate the traditional use of horses with the more obvious advantages new technology brings. These advances in science and technology which are so invaluable to the Service will have to be funded out of a budget which, if recent experience is anything to go by, will not necessarily expand to finance them. Inevitably other areas of police activity such as the Mounted Branch will be continuously scrutinised for their relevance to the Service, and value for money.

Of course, there are some members of the Constabulary who think that the maintenance of horses is a complete waste of time, and no argument can persuade them otherwise. However, I think the majority are reasonably non-committal about the whole idea; being mostly fair-minded people, they would not be for or against police horses until some evidence presented itself to persuade them one way or the other. It seemed to me that, when criticism of the Branch was levelled, it was generally without the experience of actually working with the animals on an operation, or through ignorance of our policies and procedures. I do not advance this argument as a criticism but merely as an impression I have gained.

The most important man to convince of the value of maintaining

police horses is, of course, the Chief Constable. In the end his decisions about the shape of his Force and its resources are the decisions which count, and we have been fortunate in Avon and
Somerset that Chief Constables down the century have been largely supportive - none more so than the recent incumbent, Mr David
Shattock. Being an intelligent and practical man, he would not permit the continuance of a mounted unit that was not pulling its
weight or being "value for money". Although as a horse-lover he
would have been inclined to maintain the Section, he also needed
to be convinced of its practicality and efficiency. It is true that the
unit was reduced under his Chief Constableship, but in a time of
severe financial restraint he still felt the unit to be worth preserving, albeit in a slimmer form.

So why would he, or any other Chief Constable, maintain
mounted sections as we cross the divide into the 21st century? I
think the answer lies in the introduction to this book. No matter
how old-fashioned it sounds, the maintenance of "the Queen's
Peace" still falls to the lot of the police, and the control of large
gatherings of people in public places remains a primary police
responsibility. Science may in the future develop a weapon that
stops law-breakers in their tracks without interfering with the innocent or inquisitive, but the likelihood is that it will not. Hopefully
weapons of violence will never be an acceptable option for use
against a crowd in this country, and expensive lumps of machinery
such as water cannon are insufficiently mobile and too unwieldy
for regular practical use, even if such gadgets were acceptable here.
In addition, they have no alternative application to make their
maintenance more worthwhile. So one is left with the use of the
horse. The century has demonstrated the advantages and benefits of
such use, and the involvement of horses generally has the desired
effect of halting a crowd while leaving them options of retreat. The
Mounted Section's other duties, though important and sometimes
vital, could be achieved by officers on foot or in the car - although
for some operations without mounted involvement many more officers would be needed. The function of the supervision of large bodies of people alone justifies the unit's existence.

As the new century progresses, policing may well become more
a matter of science and possibly more impersonal. As a result, it
may become even more important for the police service to main-

tain good relations with the public they are seeking to serve, and the existence of a small mounted unit, such as the one in Avon and Somerset, would help towards the continuance of such good relations, especially in a nation with a general fondness for horses. I believe that although it is essential today to have the police and public "on the same side", it will become even more vital as the years progress, and any feature of police life which enhances the relationship should be encouraged.

Although it is obvious that I can hardly speak as a dispassionate observer, I believe that, mainly for the reasons outlined above, the Mounted Branch does have a role to play in the police force of the future. These particular duties underline what really is the strength of the horse; it is a powerful animal which can oppose illegal disorder and still be gentle and attractive to small children on a school visit. Both these features of police work highlight for me, at least, the abiding qualities of the police horse. Long may they continue to serve!

The Mounted Section of the Avon and Somerset Constabulary pictured at Ashton Court

APPENDIX I

OFFICERS OF THE
MOUNTED SECTION IN CENTENARY YEAR,
WITH DATE OF JOINING SECTION:
(PHOTOGHAPHS BY SHIRLEY YEATMAN)

Sergeant Andrew Bishop (1997)

PC Ian Hull (1983)

PC Darryl Snow (1985)

PC Derek Tate (1987)

WPC Louise Smith (1988)

PC Jonathan Green (1990)

WPC Shirley Yeatman (1992)

WPC Kerry Nichols (1994)

PC Ian West (1995)

PC Ted Grabowski (1997)

WPC Tracey Small (1997)

WPC Helen Reynolds (Temporary attachment: awaiting transfer)

APPENDIX II

POLICE HORSES WITH THE
MOUNTED SECTION IN CENTENARY YEAR

(CORRECT AT TIME OF GOING TO PRINT SEPTEMBER 1998)

		age (years)
1.	Woodspring	20
2.	Kingswood	19
3.	Taunton Deane	15
4.	Yeovil	14
5.	Northavon	10
6.	Matthew	8
7.	Venturer	7
8.	Somerset	6
9.	Imperial	6
10.	Windsor	6
11.	Remount	5

# Appendix III

Officers in charge of the
Mounted Section 1899 - 1999

1. Inspector Turner (1899 - 1914)
2. Inspector Macey (c.1909 - 1914)
3. Sergeant Bees / Sergeant Parker (1919 - 1935)
4. Sergeant Smith (later Inspector) (1935 - 1958)
5. Inspector Bradley (1958 - 1960)
6. Inspector Peters (later Chief Inspector) (1960 - 1970)
7. Chief Inspector Cheetham (1970 - 1985)
8. Chief Inspector Griffiths (1985 - 1992)
9. Sergeant Jobbins* / Sergeant Foulkes* (1992 - 1997)
10. Sergeant Bishop* (1997-)

* Under Dog Section Inspector McIver (dual responsibility for Mounted and Dog Sections)

HENRY ALLBUTT'S ORIGINAL REPORT LEADING TO THE FOUNDING OF THE MOUNTED BRANCH

17th May 1899.

Proposed Mounted Force

The Chief Constable has the honour to report that in accordance with the instructions of the Committee he has examined the saddlery used by the Police when engaged upon mounted escort duty.

The Chief Constable finds that there are only three saddles belonging to the Corporation, and twelve sets of bridles, headstalls tc., and twelve sabres.

The sabres are in fair condition but the saddlery requires renewal.

The Chief Constable would advocate the establishment of a small permanent mounted force - of four Constables, and for these plenty of employment could be found in patrol duty, and in acting as mounted orderlies in carrying dispatches

the central, and the outside
Police Stations.

This number would not
of course be sufficient for
escort duty for which the
ordinary Police would have
to be mounted as heretofore.

The Chief Constable could
provide these four men without
asking for any increase of
the Force. If the mounted branch
were made larger he would
have to ask for extra men.

But whether a permanent
mounted branch be established
or not the Chief Constable would
strongly recommend that new
saddlery and appointments for
one Officer, and eight men be
purchased, so that when an
escort is turned out, it may not
present the discreditable appearance
which it does at present

H Allbutt
C.C.

Picture Acknowledgements

The photographs in this book are reproduced courtesy of the following:

Avon and Somerset Constabulary: Pages 12, 19, 21, 29, 31, 39, 50, 52 (lower), 53,58 (lower),73,89,92 (upper), 97, 101, 103, 104 (lower), 109, 113 (upper), 114, 120, 124 (upper), 125 (lower),134, 143, 144, 153, 154, 161 (upper & lower), 168, 172, 176, 177, 178, 184, 187
Bath Chronicle: Page 166
Mr Trevor Beck: Page 64
Mrs Grace Bradley: Pages 59, 71, 77, 83
Bristol Evening Post: Pages 155, 175
Bristol Record Office: Pages 35, 192, 193
Mr Kenneth Bush: Page 113 (lower)
Mrs Diana Davies: Page 125 (upper)
Dorset and Bournemouth Constabulary: Page 179
Mrs Doreen Evans: Pages 33,34
Mr Jeff Goslin: Page 164
Mr Jon Green: Page 181
Mr Peter Griffiths: Page 138
Mr Bill Hardacre: Page 67
Mr Gerry Haskey: Page 152
Ms Janis Hughes: Page 7
Mrs Janet Hunt: Pages 51 (lower), 58 (upper), 63, 69, 78, 68, 82, 85, 86, 94
Mr Alan Jobbins: Pages 126, 173
Mrs Phyllis Jones: Page 115
Mr James Marment: Pages 96, 133
Mr David McIver: Page 151
Mr Alan Milsom: Pages 79, 92 (lower), 99, 105, 110, 111
Mr Ivor Morris: Pages 136, 163
Mr John Nash: Pages 139, 145
Mrs Hilda Palmer: Page 47
Mrs Mary Parker: Page 52 (upper)
Mrs Linda Pitts: Pages 36, 37
Mr Philip Samson: Page 51 (upper)
Mr Frank Turner: Page 84
Jane Williams: Page 3
Shirley Yeatman: Page 189

Wherever possible, permission to reproduce the pictures in this book has been sought from the copyright holders. If there has been any inadvertent omission, please inform the publisher at Broadcast Books.

Index

Note. References to horse show awards are made under the named shows under 'horse show awards' and not to individual riders or horses.